THE
BUDDHA
AND THE
BARD

THE BUDDHA AND THE BARD

WHERE SHAKESPEARE'S STAGE MEETS BUDDHIST SCRIPTURES

LAUREN SHUFRAN

MANDALA

SAN RAFAEL LOS ANGELES LONDON

Contents

"ALL THE MEN AND WOMEN MERELY PLAYERS": INHABITING THE STAGE

There's no greater mark of William Shakespeare's enduring prominence than that the generic noun *bard*—a poet, a composer of verse—stands in for a single figure when preceded by a definite article. *The* Bard is Shakespeare. The word *bard* comes from the Celtic *bardo*, which serendipitously sounds just like an important Tibetan word. In Tibetan Buddhism, *bardo* is the intermediate state between death and rebirth, or more broadly interpreted, *any* interval between two states, the gaps that disturb our sense of continuity. This book sits in one such gap: between "literature" and "scripture," "embodied drama" and "transcendent practice." It plays in the geographical and temporal gaps—4,400 miles, 2,000 years—between Siddhartha Gautama's (*the* Buddha's) ancient India and Shakespeare's early modern England.

Part of that play is *closing* those gaps: placing the Buddha and the Bard beside each other and striking the gong where they touch, ears wide open to the resonances, the ways they illumine each other. Granted, this book reads Shakespeare *toward* Buddha for a distillation and illumination of Buddhism's core doctrines. And of course, we can't sidestep the fact that

Shakespeare's plays were informed by place, so there's a more or less Christian version of human nature and human experience that pervades them. So rather than "seeking out" Buddhism in Shakespeare's plays, this book begins with two basic premises: (1) Shakespeare understood human nature—perhaps especially its sufferings—better than any writer of his time; he was the dramatic master of the human condition, and (2) As for the Buddha, he saw how to *liberate* us from that condition.

What awakens at that surprising threshold between the dramatic representation of a predicament and *liberation* from it? What's the "inhabited poem" that arises where Shakespeare's words and the Buddha's wisdoms meet? How does it play out *within* us, as practice? As sources of wisdom that expand out into questions about the meaning of life, how might Shakespeare's plays reflect core Buddhist tenets or elucidate Buddhist principles through their characters? What do Buddhist views about impermanence (*anicca*), ignorance (*avijjā*), or sympathetic joy (*muditā*) kindle in our readings of the Bard? And yet still: *Why* include Shakespeare in a book about Buddhism?

There's a long history in spiritual traditions of the theater serving as a metaphor for human incarnation and spiritual practice. Buddhist psychotherapist Mark Epstein describes mindfulness (a central Buddhist practice) as "watching or feeling everything that unfolds in the theater of the mind and body."[1] American spiritual teacher Ram Dass describes spiritual work as coming to "understand that you are a soul passing through a life in which the entire drama is a script for your awakening and that you are

---

1 Mark Epstein, *The Trauma of Everyday Life* (New York: Penguin Books, 2013), 28.

more than just the drama. You are a spiritual being having a human experience."[2] Elsewhere, he quotes the third-century philosopher Plotinus in underscoring how, through spiritual awakening, life becomes "a pageant, a play":

> All must be considered as so much stage-show, so many shiftings of scenes, the horror and outcry of a play. For here, too, in all the changing doom of life, it is not the true man, the inner soul, that grieves or laments, but merely the phantasm of the man, the outer man, playing his part on the boards [stage] of the world.[3]

Shakespeare recognized the inherent theatricality of existence, our ephemeral fictionality, long before the West caught up to him. "All the world's a stage, / And all the men and women merely players," he has Jacques claim in *As You Like It*. Unlike his contemporary playwrights, Shakespeare was an actor before he was a dramatist: in the practice of emptying himself of himself, night after night, to become another *persona* (a word which refers to both the mask worn by an actor and the part one plays in a drama). Acting demands an attitude that's vast as space, that can enter into another's subjectivity and share their interiority, that makes room for all forms of experience. In all his emptying and filling—the theatrical *bardos*, the gaps between personas, the vast spaciousness in which he unbecame himself to become someone other—surely

2 Ram Dass, *Polishing the Mirror: How to Live from Your Spiritual Heart* (Boulder: Sounds True, 2014), 7.

3 Ram Dass, *Paths to God: Living the Bhagavad Gita* (New York: Harmony Books, 2004), 62.

Shakespeare began to perceive what Buddhism understands as the root of our suffering: that we are *persons* and *personas* (temporary individuals and transient players) who earnestly believe we're permanent *selves*. What Shakespeare seems to have understood—or at least, what he has Jacques *say*—is that there *is* no unchanging essence called "I." "I am not what I am," Shakespeare has Iago acknowledge in *Othello*. "Thus play I in one person many people," he has Richard II observe. Buddhism calls this, one of its fundamental doctrines, *anatta.*

We could strike the gong again and again—as this book will do—percussing Buddhist wisdoms with Shakespearean ones:

"Thinking makes good and bad." (Wonhyo)[4]

"There is nothing either good or bad but thinking makes it so." (*Hamlet*)

"In emptiness there is no form, feeling, cognition, formation, or consciousness . . . no suffering, no accumulating, no extinction, and no Way." (The Heart Sutra)[5]

"All form is formless, order orderless." (*King John*)

"Gazing at this place of nothingness," see that there are "neither eyes, ears, tongue, or body, but only dust." ("The Dust Contemplation")[6]

---

4 Emily Mark, "Wonhyo," *World History Encyclopedia*, accessed August 11, 2021, https://www.worldhistory.org/Wonhyo/.

5 "Translations of The Heart Sutra," DharmaNet International, accessed August 11, 2021, https://www.dharmanet.org/HeartSutra.htm.

6 Eric M. Greene, "The Dust Contemplation: A Study and Translation of a Newly Discovered Chinese Yogācāra Meditation Treatise from the Haneda Dunhuang Manuscripts of the Kyo-U Library," *Eastern Buddhist* 48, no. 2 (2017): 12.

"Golden lads and girls all must, / As chimney-sweep-ers, come to dust. . . . The sceptre, learning, physic, must / All follow this, and come to dust." (*Cymbeline*)

Touch Shakespeare to Siddhartha over and over again, and a series of insights emerge that feel increasingly poignant for the gap between them. "We" are radical contractions of our much vaster being. The embodied drama we're living is only part of the truth. We are infinitely more spacious than the phenomena we experience in these bodies, with their small stories and their changing emotions.

Yet I suspect that one of the more astonishing things Shake-speare has to teach us is that we have to touch the drama of *this* particular life more deeply if we hope to discover that, as Buddhism tells it, we are more than it. This book also rests on the evident premise—as does Buddhism—that we've *taken form*. We have bodies, personalities, tendencies, and behaviors (*saṅkhāras*, mental and emotional patterns or conditioning) that we're capable of waking up to, observing and understand-ing, and then seeing *beyond*. We have qualities, such as the capacity for infinite love and compassion, that we have yet to even understand. The reverberations that follow aren't about transcending the world, however "unreal," in which we live. They're about recognizing that the very bodies we're in, with all their aches, attachments, resistances, and pleasures, are exactly what we ought to attend to if we want to inhabit our roles as though they really matter—if we want to feel most alive during our short act on this miraculous stage that holds it all, from bliss to despair. We're a divine nobodyness that's rather wonderfully become a "somebody" with a distinct life to live. And we are our *own* gateways back to the sacred if we can fully connect with that life, using our circumstances to answer the question—which is *Hamlet*'s opening line—"Who's there?" Shakespeare opens us to the possibility that "I" is infinitely more capacious than this body. And yet Buddhism teaches us that embodiment is a curriculum for learning to live in freedom.

For centuries, there's been a powerful sense among readers, critics, directors, and theatergoers that Shakespeare taught us to understand ourselves by reading us so definitively—that he demonstrates us to ourselves through characters that both *reflect* us and show us what's *possible* in us. In 1765, the poet, essayist, and critic Samuel Johnson maintained that Shakespeare's greatness lay in his ability to "hold up to his readers a faithful mirror of manners and of life" through his "just representations" of human nature.[7] In 1818, critic and essayist William Hazlitt claimed that Shakespeare was "all that others were, or that they could become . . . he had only to think of any thing in order to become that thing."[8] Literary critic Harold Bloom claimed in 1998 that Shakespeare remains so steadfastly at the center of the canon because he read us better than we'll ever read *him*: "Shakespeare will go on explaining us, in part because he invented us."[9] Shakespearean editor John Wilders describes "Shakespeare's uniquely copious

7 Manpreet Kaur Anand, *An Overview of Hamlet Studies* (Cambridge: Cambridge Scholars Publishing, 2019), 7.
8 "Hazlitt's Lectures on the English Poets," *Weekly Repertory, Or Literary Gazette* 3, no. 2 (1818): 123.
9 Harold Bloom, *Shakespeare: The Invention of the Human* (New York: Riverhead Books, 1998), xviii.

powers of empathy, his capacity not simply to understand people unlike himself but in his imagination to become them."[10]

But the writer who perhaps understood Shakespeare most *spiritually* was Jorge Luis Borges, who wrote that "there was no one in him: behind his face [*persona*] . . . only . . . a dream dreamt by no one." What drew Shakespeare to the theater, Borges suggests, was his "emptiness," the urgency (or was it the *play*?) of "simulating that he was someone, so that others would not discover his condition as no one." Occasionally, Borges proposes, the Bard would hide confessions in his plays—Iago's "I am not what I am" speaks more for his creator than for his character—but mostly he was satisfied pretending to *be* someone before crowds of persons who'd pretend to *take* him for that person. "No one has ever been so many men as this man," Borges claims. And when Shakespeare finds himself in the presence of God—"before or after dying," Borges writes, offering the possibility that the Bard touched God while still alive—*his* creator tells him: "I have dreamt the world as you dreamt your work, my Shakespeare, and among the forms in my dream are you, who like myself are many and no one."[11]

Buddhism tells us that we, like Borges's Shakespeare and his God, are "many and no one," everything and nothing, emptiness and the totality of what is. Our Buddha Nature (*tathāgatagharba*), that which realizes this, is already right here, within us. We need only awaken to it. Both Shakespeare and the

....
10 William Shakespeare, *Antony and Cleopatra*, ed. John Wilders (London: The Arden Shakespeare, 2006), 42.

11 Jorge Luis Borges, "Everything and Nothing," trans. J. E. Irby, accessed August 11, 2021, http://www.friendsofcoleridge.com/MembersOnly/Clayson_Ramsgate_files/borges.htm.

Buddha begin with the body, with "character," with form, with ordinary life. They offer models for how to inquire within, how to become acute readers of ourselves: our love, greed, anger, loneliness, jealousy, passion. Even as Shakespeare's most spiteful villains wreak havoc through his plays (think Iago, or Richard III, or *King Lear*'s Edmund), each time they break the fourth wall to speak to us, we're startled by both the depth of their self-awareness and their honesty with us. They know something about themselves that we, in our very full, loud, and restless lives, often don't. And so we learn to read ourselves better by reading them.

In the yogic tradition ubiquitous in Siddhartha's India, this line of inquiry is called *svādhyāya*, self-study. *Svādhyāya* ultimately encourages these questions: What are our patterns of attraction and repulsion, like and dislike, *rāga* and *dosa*? What phenomena trigger our anger, our agitation, our jealousy, our joy, our fear? What is the source and the nature of our suffering? *Where* are we ignorant and *of what*, and what's that ignorance causing us to miss—or convincing us *exists* when it *doesn't*? Where is our behavior out of integrity with our values? How can we be our most compassionate, open-hearted, equanimous selves in the roles—kings, jesters, dukes, magicians, servants, abbesses, fools—we've been handed? *How*, on the other hand, do we remember that we're ultimately *not* those roles after all? And what kind of "play" remains after that Great Remembering?

Neither Buddhist practices nor reading Shakespeare are passive undertakings. But they're both tender and potent arts that help us live better. This book is an experiment in practicing both *together*, and while its formal structure is guided by Buddhist principles, each chapter (or, if you will, each meditation) leads with a Shakespearean epigraph as a lens through which to illuminate that principle. Finally, there are many close readings of the Bard's language here, because the rigor-and-ritual of coming in close to inquire into the nuances of a text is a way of cultivating broader forms of aliveness and attention. Attention is transformative. It, too, is a practice, but it's also a form of love. It's ultimately what spiritualizes any experience.

A brief note on terminology and textual editions. There are two main Buddhist traditions: the Mahāyāna—mostly practiced in the Northern Asian countries of Bhutan, China, Japan, Korea, and Tibet, but also in Vietnam—and the Theravāda, practiced in the South Asian countries of Cambodia, Laos, Myanmar, Sri Lanka, and Thailand. While I've drawn on literature from both traditions, the primary scriptures I quote are mainly from the Pāli canon, the tradition studied and practiced in the Theravāda lineage. For this reason, throughout the book, all foreign-language Buddhist terminology is in Pāli unless otherwise noted. Transliteration is made in accordance with A. P. Buddhadatta Mahāthera's *Concise Pāli-English Dictionary*, with reference also made to the Pāli Text Society's *Pāli-English Dictionary*. As for Shakespeare, I've leaned on the Norton edition (ed. Stephen Greenblatt et al.), which is based on the authoritative 1986 Oxford edition.

Here's to remembering where (and who) we were before we arrived on this stage—and to touching the mystery that preceded your play's first line.

Blessings on your journey, friends.

INTO THE PRACTICE

TAKING PLACE, KEEPING WATCH: VIGILANCE IN *1 HENRY VI*

. . . take your places and be vigilant.

—*1 HENRY VI*, ACT 2, SCENE 1

This line is an order from a nameless French Sergeant, speaking to two sentinels at the fortifications before the town of Orléans. It's the scene's opening line, which means it comes fresh, and loudly, off the stage silence of a scene change (like it arrives into the stilled space after the preface of this book). It's also a deceptively simple directive—"guard diligently"—in the midst of a siege. The command is met with grumbling: "Thus are poor servitors . . . Constrained to watch in darkness, rain, and cold," the First Sentinel sourly protests as the Sergeant exits. So while they outwardly observe the *first* half of the command, the sentinels ultimately fail to appreciate the Sergeant's instruction in its entirety. They're *in place* but deficient in vigilance—literally "not on their guard" when the

English forces arrive with scaling ladders. And as the English scale the ramparts from all sides, the French have no choice but to scramble over the walls, half-dressed. Some editions of the play characterize the fleeing men as "half ready and half unready" in their stage directions: a state of affairs that may feel familiar in the array of life events that besiege us—not to mention those we freely invite inside.

In the quarrel over responsibility that follows the attack, the French soldiers' claim that each of their shares of the wall was "secure" ("mine was secure," claims the Bastard of Orléans after his escape; "and so was mine," René quickly adds) is a play on the word. *Secure* had only meant "protected from danger," and therefore well defended, for about a decade when Shakespeare used it here. The word had a longer history of signifying complacency and carelessness. So while the French sentinels believe they're defending themselves (*my share of the wall was diligently guarded*), their language unknowingly acknowledges their failures to stay heedful (*I was careless with my share of the wall*).

What I love about the Sergeant's command as it pertains to spiritual practice is the holistic significance of *both* its parts, taken together: *first* take your place, *then* be vigilant. Indeed, it's among the more remarkable calls to practice I've seen in Shakespeare. Take yoga, which—like the Buddha's teachings—emerged from the spiritual wellspring of ancient India. Today we think of *asanas* as the extensive catalogue of ways yogis contort their bodies. But when Patañjali used the word in his Yoga Sutras, he was referring to the position in which one sits for the practices of *prāṇāyāma* (breath control) and *dhāraṇā* (concentrative meditation). Literally translated, *asana* means "to take one's seat"—in the Sergeant's words, to *take one's place*: set oneself in a position to go inward, take a posture from which to observe-and-know oneself, make of oneself a hushed and miniature cosmos in which to make contact with oneself. In contemporary practice this *could* be outward (a literal seat taken for meditation), but it *must* be inward (the metaphorical seat the mind takes in order to *see* itself).

There's a contemporary enthusiasm for meditation's relaxing—and even sleep-inducing—effects. But traditional Buddhist texts emphasized *vigilant wakefulness* as a means of shifting perception: the transformed understanding of reality that led to awakening. The Pāli term is *appamāda*, a negation of *pamāda* (heedless). *Appamāda* is the heed*ful* application of diligence to all one's activities. As the taking-of-profound-care concerning what should be avoided, and what cultivated, in every moment, *appamāda* is the source of all virtuous qualities. The Appamāda Sūtra tells us that "all skillful qualities are rooted in heedfulness, converge in heedfulness, and heedfulness is reckoned the foremost among them."[12] Through vigilance—the incessant watch of the sentinel who's watching *themselves*—we uncover what Tibetan Buddhist nun Pema Chödrön calls "our growing understanding of what truly helps and harms us."[13] This is true regardless of whether we're taking

---

12 "Appamada Sutta: Heedfulness," AN 10.15, Access to Insight, last modified November, 30, 2013, http://www.accesstoinsight.org/tipitaka/an/an10/an10.015.than.html.
13 Pema Chödrön, *No Time to Lose: A Timely Guide to the Way of the Bodhisattva* (Boston: Shambhala, 2005), 118.

place (*asana*) on a meditation cushion, or in our cars, or in every next comment in our conversations. And here's where the word *asana* marvelously resonates with the word *besiege* (literally, "*to sit down* before a place in order to capture it"): in routinely sitting and facing ourselves, we actively catch and transform what would otherwise harm us. If there's a moral in this assemblage of words, it's that *sitting* is an alive and dynamic act.

What the French sentinels and Buddhist texts offer us is the meaningfulness of *the watch*—not of the anxious or defensive kind (as one has in war), but a watching that's buoyed by an undercurrent of curiosity and self-compassion. *Without* vigilant wakefulness, unwholesome mental states (*kilesas*)— such as anger, greed, stubbornness, and arrogance—arise and cloud the mind, scaling our undefended ramparts from all sides like Shakespeare's English soldiers, manifesting in unskillful actions because we were half-unready to *meet* them when they arrived. But when we bring courageous energy and wide-awake exertion to our moment-to-moment existence, the less likely those mental states are to find some weakly guarded spot along our walls. What's more, we're guarded *against* sleeping through life—because we've taken a place of spirited persistence.

So while it's a wartime instruction, the Sergeant's words are worth internalizing—and worth commencing this book with. Taking a position, getting into a posture, finding a site from *within* oneself and *before* oneself to practice vigilance is to constantly (re-)locate the most skillful place to live *in*, and live *out*, each moment. It makes us less *besieged* and more thoughtfully *besieging*. And it invites us to a more active reception of the Bard's words and the Buddha's teachings.

"OUR BODIES ARE OUR GARDENS": IAGO ON CULTIVATING SEEDS

Our bodies are our gardens, to the which our wills are gardeners; so that if we will plant nettles or sow lettuce, set hyssop and weed up thyme, supply it with one gender of herbs or distract it with many, either to have it sterile with idleness or manured with industry, why, the power and corrigible authority of this lies in our wills.

—*OTHELLO*, ACT 1, SCENE 3

It's easy to forget that *Othello* is a play of more than one heartbreak. Roderigo is in love with Desdemona, who's eloped with Othello, leaving the unrequited lover in a state of jealous despair. Desdemona's father brings his grievance over the secret marriage to the Duke, claiming the African general must have "enchanted" his daughter "with foul charms." In the hearing that follows, Othello eloquently recounts how Desdemona fell in

23

love with him, Desdemona professes her loyalty to her new husband, and she asks to accompany him on his next military venture so as not to be denied sexual intimacy: "If I be left behind . . . the rites for why I love him are bereft me." It's a remarkably forthright request; and as the stage clears, leaving Iago and Roderigo—who've witnessed these public declarations of love—one imagines the miserable lover visualizing the marital "rites" Desdemona openly craves. "I will incontinently drown myself," he claims melodramatically, evoking Iago's frustration. "I confess it is my shame to be so fond, but it is not in my virtue to amend it." But Iago rejects the notion that Roderigo is emotionally impotent. "'Tis in ourselves that we are thus or thus," he counters. We're beings *abundant* in agency, like farmers over their fields; and it's through our actions ("planting," "weeding," "manuring"), or lack thereof ("idleness"), that we are one thing or another.

Granted, this assertion by the play's villain is troubling in context: Iago's conviction that one can make whatever one "wills" is intricately tied to his puppeteering of the tragedy by directing its characters to do as he wants. Yet it holds the seeds of a deeper wisdom when self-directed. Through the metaphor of the body-garden, Iago reminds us to be conscientious about *what* we plant there, and diligent in tending to it once it's in our ground. The horticultural metaphor refuses the theory that character and emotion are beyond our realm of influence. Rather, one can both *cultivate* and *weed out* aspects of self in order to live more skillfully.

It's a familiar metaphor in Buddhism. The Pāli word for meditation is *bhāvanā*, which literally means "cultivation": to prepare soil for crops, to till, to tend the terrain. Farmers perform *bhāvanā* when they plant seeds. When the Buddha chose this metaphor for meditation practice, it was in context of the ubiquitous fields of his native India. But it's a metaphor that serves just as well in our contemporary, steel-and-concrete world because it invites us to think about everything from agency, to habitual patterns, to patience.

Buddhism's aim is the ethical cultivation of oneself *by oneself*, the development of mind and action through one's own (right) efforts. In self-cultivation, the practitioner is both garden and gardener. Buddhism uses another horticultural metaphor to describe how previous thoughts and actions leave unconscious karmic traces that influence our *future* thoughts and actions. It calls these *bīja*, "seeds," and they're a valuable metaphor for cognitive conditioning. As Buddhist scholar Dan Lusthaus writes, "just as plants reproduce only their own kind, so do wholesome or unwholesome karmic acts produce effects after their own kind."[14] "When I perform an action motivated by greed," Rupert Gethin elaborates in *The Foundations of Buddhism*, "it plants a 'seed' in . . . my mind. Such a seed is not a thing in itself . . . [but] in the course of time . . . [it] matures and issues a particular result, in the same way as a seed does not produce its fruit immediately."[15]

"You have many good seeds of happiness and joy in you," writes Vietnamese Buddhist monk Thich Naht Hanh (Thay).

---

14 Dan Lusthaus, "Vasubandhu," accessed August 1, 2021, http://www.acmuller.net/yogacara/thinkers/vasubandhu.html.
15 Rupert Gethin, *The Foundations of Buddhism* (Oxford: Oxford University Press, 1998), 222.

"You have the seed of compassion, of understanding, of love in you, and you practice in order to get in touch with appropriate attention."[16] "Appropriate attention" is a phrase that softly resounds for me. It's a tenderer version of Iago's assertion that "the power and corrigible [correctable] authority . . . lies in our wills" in the face of Roderigo's claim that he can't "amend" himself; he's helplessly destined to suffer in love. Both Buddhism and Iago maintain that we only produce suffering *gardens* if we plant suffering *seeds*. "That's the law of retribution," explains Thay. "A good act will bring a good result. So the seed of corn only manifests as a plant of corn, and not something else."[17] What springs from the ground of us shouldn't surprise us, especially if we've consciously planted it there. Unfortunately, however, we often *un*consciously scatter seeds. And we're shocked when they then bear undesirable fruit.

When we begin to develop an awareness of the law of *kamma* (cause and effect), we observe karmic habits, the seeds of our own farming, sprouting as new-yet-familiar experiences. They produce more fruit with more seeds that bloom into actions and cognitions that resemble the *last* ones. And when thoughts and actions—whether wholesome or unwholesome—become habits, *that's* a field of being we're wholly responsible for. Or, as Iago would say, it was in our "authority" all along.

The Tibetan word for meditation—*gom*—is deeply linked with the word for "habit." In the Tibetan language, in other words, to

16 Thich Naht Hanh, "Dharma Talk: The Power of Visualization," Mindfulness Bell, accessed August 1, 2021, https://www.mindfulnessbell.org/archive/tag/Eight+ Levels+of+Consciousness.
17 Hanh, "Dharma Talk."

meditate is to habituate: to cultivate Thay's "seeds of happiness and joy" through skillful, repeated action. *Whatever* our chosen practice, the aim is to routinely inquire into *which* thoughts and actions we want multiplied, propagating our ground. The garden metaphor invites us into the meaningfulness of patience: we cultivate healing and growth as seeds do—*in time*. It also reminds us that practice is as much about uprooting the *undesirable* weeds as it is about nurturing the *desired* herbs and flowers. Which means it can, at times, feel endless. Until we reach full awakening, weeds born of craving, hatred, and ignorance (*rāga*, *dosa*, and *moha*) will return. This is simply the nature of things. So we must not only be *constant* but also *compassionate*, knowing that weeds are a natural consequence of the existence of ground.

But we must also remember that, in time, this constant, compassionate, gradual process of gardening the field-of-our-being will yield more and more flowers, fewer and fewer weeds. "Just do your daily practice," Tibetan Buddhist nun Thubten Chodron advises: "Abandon impatience and instead be content creating the causes for goodness; the results will come when they're ready."[18] It's a description of farming at its finest—not only *forgiving* of time but satisfied *in* it, "content in creating." What are the names of the seeds we want to cultivate *more* of in our remarkably rich and fecund and full-of-possibility body gardens? What are the weeds we must clear for those new *bīja* to spaciously grow, and multiply, and thrive?

---

18 "Meditator's Toolbox: 21 Tips to Power Your Practice," Tricycle, accessed August 4, 2021, https://tricycle.org/magazine/meditators-toolbox/.

BECOMING STRANGE
TO THE WORLD:
TROILUS AND CRESSIDA
AND BEGINNER'S MIND

And here to do you service am become
As new into the world, strange, unacquainted.

—*TROILUS AND CRESSIDA*, ACT 3, SCENE 3

In the early days of the Trojan War, Calchas—Cressida's father and a Trojan priest—defects to the Greek camp because he prophesies Troy's downfall. The daughter he leaves behind falls in love with a Trojan named Troilus. But on the very night the lovers consummate their union, Calchas is visiting the Greek commander Agamemnon to persuade him to release a Trojan prisoner in exchange for Cressida: the traitor longs to be reunited, *in Greece*, with the daughter he abandoned. So after a single night together, the lovers are separated. These lines form part of the logic Calchas uses to bargain with Agamemnon for his daughter. He reminds the general how much he risked (notably, *everything*) when he abandoned Troy for Greece: "[I] left my profession, / Incurred a traitor's name, exposed myself . . . to doubtful fortunes, sequest'ring from me all . . . most familiar to my nature." It's a claim of radical estrangement-from-self, a renouncing of all that had preserved his identity. And it was "to do you service," Calchas reminds Agamemnon, that he's "become / As new into the world, strange, unacquainted." Paradoxically, the "recompense" Calchas wants for *relinquishing* all that once affirmed his identity is reunion with a daughter who'd served as one of those affirmations. The moral of Calchas's request? Identity dies hard.

In a play that depicts a handful of legendary characters who fail to uphold their mythic qualities and become, instead, undignified versions of themselves (among Shakespeare's source texts for *Troilus and Cressida* was the ancient Greek epic poem *The Iliad*), Calchas's description of having pulled the rug out from under his own identity is arresting. Granted, the priest's becoming-strange to himself occurs in the context of betrayal. But as we've already seen, some of Shakespeare's most unpleasant characters deliver his wisest lines. And when I wrest this line from the play and apply it to my encounters with the world, it thoroughly changes their tenor.

When I am *not* "new" or "strange" or "unacquainted" with the world, I'm approaching it with stubborn conviction about the story I tell of *myself* and of *it*, seeking out the ways it confirms "who I am" in my own narrow, delimited Troy. I move through it in ways that express the beliefs and opinions I've already self-affirmed, that assert and strengthen my attachments. I pursue people and situations that validate myself. I'm disappointed when those things prove inconstant, because *their* inconstancy announces the unreliability of my own selfhood. My attention adheres to what I identify as belonging to me: *my* thoughts and emotions, *my* body, *my* qualities and abilities, *my* work, words, possessions, relationships, impressions, sensations, successes. And because I've made myself the center of experience, there's no real intimacy with the world and those *in* it—I'm too busy defending "I" to show up for what's actually *there*.

In his essay "Genjōkōan," thirteenth-century Zen master Dōgen writes: "To study Buddhism is to study the self. To study the self is to forget the self. To forget the self is to be enlightened by all things."[19] For Dōgen—as for the Buddha—self-study involved turning attention toward our direct experiences as living beings. Through meditation and mindfulness practices—ardent watchings-of-ourselves—we discover how changeable we are; how, moment to moment, we really *are* "strange" and "new." We witness thoughts, feelings, and emotions come and go—sometimes in a matter of seconds. We begin to notice gaps in what we once perceived as enduring, continuous selves. *This* is the beginning of self-forgetting, and it requires getting *intimate* with ourselves before we become "unacquainted." (Dōgen uses the word *narau* for

19 Dogen, "Genjokoan," trans. Reiho Masunaga, The Zen Site, accessed August 4, 2021, http://www.thezensite.com/ZenTeachings/Dogen_Teachings/GenjoKoan8.htm#clr0.

"study." It's related to *neraru*: "to become familiar with." This is one of Buddhism's delightful paradoxes: becoming-strange by becoming-familiar.)

When we cease to see the world as a collection of persons and events that validate who we think we are, *every* sense awakens to experience, keenly and penetratingly. *Every* encounter we have with it becomes astonishing, instructive, revealing—which is what Dōgen meant when he said "to forget the self is to become enlightened by all things." When we're new to the world—having shed what Buddhist psychology calls "the thicket of views and opinions"—we experience what Zen Buddhists call *shoshin*, "beginner's mind."[20] In his classic work *Zen Mind, Beginner's Mind*, Zen master Shunryu Suzuki writes, "If your mind is empty, it is always ready for anything; it is open to everything. In the beginner's mind there are many possibilities; in the expert's mind there are few."[21]

Without our "expert" expectations, indoctrinations, theories, biases, beliefs (the "profession" Calchas forsook meant both "vocation" and "declaration of belief")—indeed, without *ourselves*—nothing remains to staunchly defend. There's no room for disappointment, because in the new there's no expectation. All experience becomes curiosity and wonder. We approach others without prejudgment, hearts and eyes cracked open with awe. And true intimacy is now possible, because we're listening as though hearing for the first time.

....
20 Jack Kornfield, "The Beauty of Beginner's Mind," accessed August 4, 2021, https://jackkornfield.com/beginners-mind/.
21 Shunryu Suzuki, *Zen Mind, Beginner's Mind*. ed. Trudy Dixon (New York: Weatherhill, 1995), 21.

When I read Calchas's lines, the undercurrent of infidelity to the polis falls away, and "doing you service" becomes about the radical transformation of relationship that's possible when we arrive at each other *so* familiar with ourselves that we've forgotten identity, become new. *This* is the grounds of true intimacy. If nothing needs to verify us any longer, we can let it be wholly what it is. We arrive at each other undone, available to awe. "Service" has, at its roots, a sense of worship—a bowing to what is. How might we begin to "unacquaint" ourselves from ourselves so we can better serve and honor the world as it is?

The Three Marks of Existence

IMPERMANENCE AND PROSPERO'S MASQUE

These our actors,
As I foretold you, were all spirits, and
Are melted into air, into thin air;
And like the baseless fabric of this vision,
The cloud-capped towers, the gorgeous palaces,
The solemn temples, the great globe itself,
Yea, all which it inherit, shall dissolve;
And, like this insubstantial pageant faded,
Leave not a rack behind. We are such stuff
As dreams are made on, and our little life
Is rounded with a sleep.

—THE TEMPEST, ACT 4, SCENE 1

Prospero is the protagonist, sorcerer, and puppet master of *The Tempest*. He was once Duke of Milan, but he was usurped by his brother Antonio, who forced him and his infant daughter into "a rotten carcass" of a boat one night and sent them helplessly off to sea. Prospero and Miranda have been living on an island ever since; but when a ship carrying Antonio appears on their horizon one day, Prospero creates a tempest to destroy it and bring his brother to shore. And so begins a revenge play whose theme is ultimately forgiveness. Ferdinand—son of the King of Naples, who aided Antonio in unseating his brother—is among the shipwrecked; he and Miranda fall in love at first sight. Prospero initially accuses Ferdinand of feigning royalty and puts him to work hauling wood. But as Ferdinand performs his labor with lightness, Prospero softens and becomes willing to celebrate their betrothal. He does so with a masque—a lavish courtly dance. Spirits are summoned to assume the shapes of various goddesses, who bless the couple. The entire performance is an extraordinary display of power that leaves Ferdinand in awe.

But at the height of the performance and the lovers' wonder, Prospero remembers something important: There's a conspiracy against his life—led by the islander Caliban and two other shipwrecked men—and "the minute of their plot / Is almost come." He abruptly sends the spirits away, demanding an end to the festivities so he can attend to his own survival. The young lovers are unsettled by Prospero's agitation, but the magician comforts them. "Be cheerful, sir," he urges Ferdinand. "Our revels now are ended." What follows is the remarkable monologue above, about the nature of theater, and of life.

The Tempest was the last play Shakespeare wrote alone, and there's something tantalizing about the thought that Prospero's speech might be a reflection on the playwright's own mortality, the impermanence of his creations, the brevity of his legacy. We who've longed to hear "Shakespeare's own voice" seek it here, signaling his relinquishment. We point to Prospero's mention of "the great globe itself" (a pun on the name of Shakespeare's theater), which—like all else—"shall dissolve." But whether or not Shakespeare intended to speak for himself here, he's given us a meditation on the essential transience of things. The speech feels all the more poignant because it's spoken by a figure whom we finally saw simply delighting in the present, *without* the weight of vengeance propelling his actions. We've just experienced Prospero in his fullest nature, surprisingly forgetful of the business of real life—indeed, the work of staying alive.

The speech insists upon both the exquisite artistry of the world Prospero's created and that world's insubstantiality. An audience *sees* themselves suddenly in this invitation to contemplate their own mortality—witnessing a play that will "dissolve" in the following act, just as their own lives ultimately will. Just as the *actors'* lives will, as will every emotion that's been felt by every auditor wherever this speech has been performed, as will—in time—The Globe and the globe that contains it. Prospero's island, the theater, and the world beyond the stage converge for a moment in their fleetingness, their winged passage toward non-being, their "melting" and "dissolving." "Our little life / Is rounded with a sleep," Prospero declares, meaning our lives are bookmarked by a *different* kind of consciousness. This is perhaps my favorite line of all, because it suggests that what happens *between* sleeps—this thing we call life—is a form of wakefulness. And a wakeful life means realizing that all we experience while *in* it is "insubstantial," an illusion.

One of Buddhism's essential doctrines is the "three marks" or "three characteristics" of phenomenal existence (*tilakkhaṇa*): impermanence (*anicca*), unsatisfactoriness or suffering (*dukkha*), and non-self (*anatta*). The first of these marks is typically understood as the ground of the other two. The very *perception* of *anicca*—that all temporal things, material and cerebral, are continuously changing, and that whatever comes into existence will also dissolve—is the very foundation of Buddhist philosophy.

Over and over again, the canonical texts remind us that all conditioned things (all material phenomena) are in a continual state of flux between arising and dissolving. "Materiality is impermanent, and so are feeling, perception, formations, and consciousness," says the Majjhima Nikāya.[22] The Buddha's own last words were a reminder that "all formations are subject to dissolution; [so] attain perfection through diligence."[23] Because change and impermanence are essential characteristics of phenomenal existence, even as we point to something and say "this *is*," it's already slipping beneath the weight of that declaration. Perhaps that seems obvious, and we can certainly be cavalier about it: *Well, of course I'm going to die.* But only once we *truly* grasp impermanence can we "remov[e] all passion for material

22 "The Three Basic Facts of Existence: III. Egolessness (Anatta)," Access to Insight, last modified November 30, 2013, http://www.accesstoinsight.org/lib/authors/various/wheel202.html.

23 "The Three Basic Facts of Existence: I. Impermanence (Anicca)," Access to Insight, last modified November 30, 2013, http://www.accesstoinsight.org/lib/authors/various/wheel186.html.

existence, remov[e] all passion for becoming . . . remov[e] and abolis[h] all conceit of 'I am,'" according to the Buddha—and therefore, remove all suffering.[24] In other words, if we're still holding any attachments to this world and this life, we haven't fully comprehended it. This is hardly to say: don't enjoy the phenomenal world. It's to say: don't *depend* on it as a source of lasting, stable happiness.

Of course, impermanence sometimes forces itself upon our experience; but it's not always so evident. When we don't earnestly attend to the rise-and-fall of things, we *think* we're experiencing continuity. The "diligence" the Buddha spoke of is one of active, empirical observation. We look for *anicca* in our physical bodies, internal experiences, and worlds, interrupting that impression of continuity to perceive their brevity. A glass breaks. You walk the same path twice and observe that within a matter of days new shoots have sprouted; others have begun to wither, or turn red, or rot. Not a single color abides—or *is*— in a sunset. The body ages, becoming inadequate to the task of living. One thought replaces another, one emotion the next, in a ceaseless string of mind (and heart) chatter, until neither mind nor heart *is*. Beneath every perception is an incalculable series of alterations, occurring with such rapidity that they defy measurement. Or, to put it another way, in the very act of *being*, each thing relentlessly gives-place to something other-than-it-self. *So* much so that it can never truly be called "itself."

In "diligent" practice, we ask ourselves: "What am I see-ing right now that is not subject to non-being?"; "What have

---

24 "The Three Basic Facts of Existence: I. Impermanence (Anicca)."

I perceived or experienced today that will not pass away—indeed, that hasn't already?" And then we turn to the self who dwells amid that array of impermanences. We remember that *anicca* isn't only "out there." We, too, are destined for annihilation. The practice is *not* to run to the distractions—the phone, the television, the apps, the emails—we use to evade the observable fact that we're on the verge of non-being. It's to meditate upon the material forms, contemplating their impermanence until we *truly* see that they're fleeting—and thus, as Prospero says, "insubstantial." When we pay attention, impermanence stares us in the face from all sides. And as we stare back at it, and recognize ourselves *as* it, we become free.

Buddhist texts describe the doctrine of *anicca* through a variety of metaphors that point us back to Prospero. Material existence is like a magic trick, a mirage, a fabrication that echoes Prospero's "baseless fabric": "to [a man with good eyesight]—seeing it, observing it, and appropriately examining it—it would appear empty, void, without substance: for what substance would there be in a magic trick?"[25] At the conclusion of The Diamond Sutra (Vajracchedikā Prajñāpāramitā Sūtra), the Buddha counsels:

> All conditioned dharmas
> Are like dreams, illusions, bubbles, or shadows;
> Like drops of dew, or like flashes of lightning;
> Thusly should they be contemplated.[26]

25 "Phena Sutta: Foam," SN 22.95, Access to Insight, last modified November 30, 2013, http://www.accesstoinsight.org/tipitaka/sn/sn22/sn22.095.than.html.
26 "Vajracchedikā Prajñāpāramitā Sūtra," last modified October 30, 2020, https://en.wikisource.org/wiki/Vajracchedikā_Prajñāpāramitā_Sūtra.

In Prospero's monologue we're reminded that the masque is a dream-within-a-dream, *within a dream*. And when it's time for those spirits of *our* lives to "fade" from us (or us from *them*), we'll suffer much, much less for having foreseen that that passing was precisely in their nature, and in ours. Indeed, we might even "be cheerful"—as in Prospero's instruction to Ferdinand—that we had the opportunity to experience this magnificent, fleeting life *at all*. Because when we remember that there will never be another moment like *this* one, we're all the more likely to relish it. Joy is one of the extraordinary consequences of truly seeing *anicca*.

THE SUFFERING OF PAINFUL EXPERIENCES: KING LEAR'S BIRTH CRIES AND THE BONES OF RICHARD II

When we are born, we cry that we are come
To this great stage of fools.

—*KING LEAR*, ACT 4, SCENE 6

King Lear has recently been betrayed by his two eldest daughters and thrust into a raging storm that mirrors his internal weather: we've witnessed violent disturbances *within* and *without*. He's since been wandering the fields near Dover, where he's encountered his loyal companion, Gloucester, and Gloucester's son Edgar. The king is some combination of raving and mumbling and mad, unable to wholly recognize his friend, his white hair bedecked in a wreath of wildflowers and weeds—a perverted substitute for the royal crown. A "side-piercing sight" is how Edgar describes Lear's diminishment.

Lear swings between illogic and slivers of bitter wisdom in the dialogue that ensues. He's realized the injuriousness of his daughters' flattery ("They told me I was everything. 'Tis a lie"). He's been liberated from his delusions of power ("the thunder would not peace at my bidding"). He's recognized an essential truth about the frailty of identity ("Change places, and . . . which is the justice, which is the thief?"). "Reason in madness!" Edgar observes as Lear descends back into nonsense. But then the king offers another piercing insight, turning-philosopher to advise the recently blinded Gloucester: "Thou must be patient. We came crying hither . . . the first time that we smell the air, / We wail and cry . . . that we are come / To this great stage of fools." And while moments later Lear slips back into incoherence, this insight resonates with any of us who've been willing to track the meandering utterances of the mad-yet-penetrative king.

In context, Lear's meaning seems to be that we have two great "cries" in life: once when we're cast onstage into these bodies, cold and helpless and wailing with the intuition that we'll have to not only *suffer* fools, but also *be* one. And once again when we're ripe enough to—and conditions are such that we *must*—understand the inexorable suffering of living. Both newborns and disillusioned men, flung from their pedestals, have reason to weep for having perceived the truth of conditioned life. Of course, Buddhism would add that you don't have to be flung from *anywhere* to perceive the pervasiveness of suffering;

you'll experience it without ever descending from your pedestal (though you will, eventually, have to vacate those heights). Lear just so happened to require flinging—as Gloucester required blindness—to *see*.

If you know anything about fools in Shakespeare, you know they're often among the more shrewd and insightful characters in their respective plays (the fool in *King Lear* is no exception). Yet my favorite synonym of *fool* in *this* context is "ignorant person," because it turns us head-on into Buddhism. Of course, having recognized that suffering is an essential truth of *aliveness*—even for a king—Lear is far from ignorant at this point in the play. But he seems to discern the fool that he's been. Suffering (*dukkha*) is the central concern that Buddhism addresses. You'll find it in the Buddha's first sermon, in which he laid out the Four Noble Truths: (1) *dukkha* exists; (2) *dukkha* arises due to craving (*taṇhā*), which originates in ignorance and gives rise to rebirth; (3) it's possible to end *dukkha* through the cessation of craving; (4) by following the Noble Eightfold Path.[27]

Dukkha is commonly translated as "suffering," though that's too narrow a rendering. In English it comes off as melodramatic: very few of us would probably describe our lives as principally characterized by suffering. So consider *dukkha* more expansively: annoyance; disappointment; impatience; irritation; stress; sadness; a vague sense of unsettledness, or dissatisfaction, or unease. When you admit those less-discernible qualities into the definition, the claim that *dukkha* pervades our

45

lives begins to ring a bit more true. Buddhism separates *dukkha* into three categories: the suffering of painful experiences (birth, aging, sickness, and death), the suffering of change (that pleasant experiences are impermanent), and the suffering of conditioned reality (that subtle sense of not-quite-*it*-ness that underlies the whole of our conscious lives).

That old age, sickness, and death constitute "suffering" we can readily assent to; but "birth is suffering" (*jātipi dukkhā*) may feel more difficult to concede. We tend to think of birth as a time of wondrous celebration, a miraculous arising of being from non-being. And indeed, there's much to celebrate about emergence in a body. Yet birth is our first worldly trauma, as is evidenced by the agitation of our entrance ("the first time that we smell the air, / We wail and cry"). Consider how we turn up in a sphere with discomforts on all sides. Too much heat, then too much cold, then too much hunger. It feels good to sit down—until it hurts. It feels good to stand up—until that *also* hurts. Living is an ongoing pursuit of seeking moderately more comfort as we hurdle toward dissolution. It's no great leap, then, to appreciate why the object in Buddhism is liberation from the cycle of death and rebirth—even if rebirth has no place in your landscape of belief.

Still, we limit ourselves when we assume that by "birth is suffering," the Buddha was speaking strictly of birth into a physical body. Birth *also* refers to a mental event. As the great twentieth-century Thai Buddhist monk Buddhadasa Bhikkhu writes: "wherever there arises the mistaken idea of 'I,' the 'I' has been born; its parents are ignorance [think Lear's "fools"] and craving."[28] This false sense of self begets suffering; for as soon as we have a conception of "I," what follows is *I am, I am* not, *I have, I* don't *have, I want, I* don't *want,* and so on. These are limiting phrases that perpetuate our suffering. Yet as a mental event, we're reborn a thousand times a day—each time the idea of "I" arises in the mind.

So here we are, in bodies that necessarily experience physical suffering: heat, cold, thirst, hunger, throbbings, spasms, aches, pains. But we're also *identifying* with a self these bodies accommodate: self-laboring, self-delivering, self-conceiving again and again into the beings we've attached to, that we cling to in "foolish" ignorance. And so, Buddhadasa Bhikkhu advises, "let's not concern ourselves with the birth that follows physical death," with rebirth into the next body. We're still very much alive in *this* one, and the remarkable, present-moment truth is that life continues to deliver joys and blessings—sometimes inexhaustible ones—that blunt its pains. "Instead let us concern ourselves seriously with the birth that happens *before* physical death, the kind of birth that goes on while we are alive," the (re)birth of "I." "Let us learn to master it and the problem will be eliminated."[29] And herein lies the claim that, while Buddhism recognizes suffering as a universal truth, it's hardly a pessimistic doctrine. Rather, it insists that suffering can be eradicated— wholly and happily—from our lives.

....
28 Buddhadasa Bhikkhu, "The Danger of I (Another Kind of Birth)," Dhamma Talks, accessed August 4, 2021, https://www.dhammatalks.net/Books3/Bhikkhu_Buddhadasa_ The_Danger_of_I.htm.
29 Buddhadasa Bhikkhu, "The Danger of I."

The practice is to become aware of the "I" each time it arises in the mind. In steady awareness, we observe it when it emerges and work to shift our perception to see the world as *empty* of "I," "me," and "mine." For, according to the Buddha, if we can eliminate *mental* rebirth in this life, we can eliminate *physical* rebirth for good, across lifetimes. And whether or not rebirth resonates with you, freedom from the suffering that accompanies the idea of self in *this* life just might.

And nothing can we call our own but death,
And that small model of the barren earth
Which serves as paste and cover to our bones.

—*RICHARD II,* ACT 3, SCENE 2

King Richard of England has just returned from a war in Ireland to a string of disastrous reports concerning Henry Bolingbroke, whom Richard exiled in act 1. Broken by his son's banishment, John of Gaunt dies, and Richard seizes possession of Gaunt's estates—Bolingbroke's inheritance. Upon hearing the news, Bolingbroke assembles an army and returns from exile to reclaim his confiscated dukedom.

By the time Richard returns from Ireland, he's lost his country. His confidence in the divine right of kings—the notion that his sovereignty is appointed by God and therefore invulnerable—is shattered when a relentless series of messengers enter bearing grim news: Richard's army has dispersed; the whole of England is "armed . . . against thy majesty"; his most trusted men have been executed and "lie full low, graved in the hollow ground." Catastrophic loss, desertion, the flimsiness of God's will and the shattered illusion of a divinity that would protect him: it's enough to launch the king into one of the most despairing and eloquent monologues in all of Shakespeare. "Of comfort no man speak," Richard urges his remaining companions. "Let's talk of graves, of worms and epitaphs . . . choose executors and talk of wills." But the word *will* catches Richard as he realizes he has nothing left to bequeath: "Nothing can we call our own but death, / And that small model of the barren earth / Which serves as paste and cover to our bones."

The whole of the speech is magnificent: imagine a king besmirching his robes in the dirt beneath his companions, which is what Richard is doing as he delivers these lines. Yet what most resonates for me here is that Richard is *still* trying so desperately—so *humanly*—to possess *something.* All we can call "ours," he claims, are "our" death and the earth that will cover "our" bones. While Richard can dispense with his *role*, he can't yet dispense with his *body*: he's still attached to form. The blow to monarchical identity has allowed him to ask his companions, "How can you say to me I am a king?" But Richard still believes his flesh is *his*. It seems Shakespeare has penetrated our most tenacious attachment.

The concept of *maraṇa dukkhā* (death is suffering) feels more experientially obvious to us than *jātipi dukkhā* (birth is suffering) does. Yet it's often easier for us to acknowledge death when it happens "out there" (a plum drops from its tree, a raccoon doesn't survive its crossing-of-the-road, a distant cousin dies), or when it *looks like* transition (I am a twenty-something, or an employee, or a king . . . and now I'm not). We prefer not to acknowledge the bodily death we're hastening toward. It's an understandable by-product of duality, of being-two: we carry a vague awareness of our splendid infinitude, yet the only form of ourselves we *know* goes back into the ground to blindly and dumbly rot into vanishing. So when we speak of death, we do so in whispers. We deem it inappropriate or morbid as a topic of conversation, and we dodge children's questions about it to "protect" them. We avert our eyes from its presence; and when we *can't*, we put makeup on corpses to blunt the observable reality of their deadness. We have what religious scholar George D. Bond calls an "unexamined assumption of our own immortality"—one Richard poignantly illuminates when he claims that the earth will remember the forms "our" bones and bodies took.[30]

Buddhism takes a different view of death. In all biographies of the Buddha, the prince encountered four sights when he left his palace: a sick person, an old person, a corpse, and a renunciate. These sights—the first three of which exemplify the sufferings ordinary beings are subject to, and the last of which suggests those sufferings can be transcended through spiritual practice—are considered divine, since they prompted Siddhartha to perceive the futility of worldly concerns and seek the truth. So there's a very real sense in which the entire Buddhist path begins with a recognition of death.

Even today, Buddhist teachers recommend mindfulness of death (*maraṇasati*) practices, and it's a common form of

30 George D. Bond, "Theravada Buddhism's Meditations on Death and the Symbolism of Initiatory Death," *History of Religions* 19, no. 3 (February 1980): 243.

meditation at some monasteries to observe the progressive rotting of a corpse. (The contemplation goes something like: this *body is just like* that *decaying body; it's only in a different stage of being-body, of decomposition*.) Far from morbid, these meditations on the scarcity of time offer so many possibilities for spiritual progress—and for joy. They spur us into diligent practice. They diminish our attachment to the worldly things that cause shortsighted suffering. They soften our urge to engage in escapist activities—because there's no longer a terror to escape. They align our lives with our values because they raise the urgency of every-moment-counting. Every breath becomes infinitely precious, and wondrous, and light.

The Buddha offered a *confrontation* with death—rather than an evasion—that liberates us even from our grasp on those bones, the earth we think will hold "us," the headstone that will point to "our" memory, "our" name. He taught that only those who end clinging (*taṇhā*) in this life escape the cycle of death and rebirth, become deathless. Recognizing that death is perpetually at hand, happening in every moment *and* kept at bay only by the fragility of living, we discover both the urgency of the human predicament and the way *out* of that predicament. For those of us who haven't fully eliminated clinging—who still speak of *my* earth, *my* loved ones suffering at *my* deathbed, *my* bones, the cessation of *my* hopes and dreams, the oblivion of *my* successes—the cycle continues. And indeed, if you know the play, you know Richard continues to suffer what he must surrender. Because Shakespeare, too, recognized the power of the lingering "my."

THE SUFFERING OF CHANGE:
HERMIA'S FAILING LEGS

My legs can keep no pace with my desires.

—*A MIDSUMMER NIGHT'S DREAM*, ACT 3, SCENE 3

ere's Hermia, who's moments from falling into a deep sleep—in part due to magic, in part due to the exhaustion of *wanting*. The play's love plot is a lot to keep track of: in act 1, Hermia is loved by both Demetrius (whose love she does not reciprocate) and Lysander (her beloved). But Hermia's father has chosen *Demetrius* for his daughter, so the young lovers decide to flee. They make the mistake of trusting the secret of their elopement to Helena, who's in love with Demetrius. Hoping to ignite his love, Helena relays the plan to him. At the appointed time, Demetrius follows his beloved Hermia into the woods . . . and an enamored Helena follows him.

Four aching lovers set out into the woods: it's the narrative groundwork for a lot of conceivable turmoil. Add to *this* the

53

fact that the forest is full of fairies; and their king, Oberon, takes interest in the human drama that turns up in his realm. But after Oberon's servant Puck mistakenly "charm[s the] eyes" of the wrong "Athenian" with a love potion as he sleeps (it's worth noting the relationship between desire and fatigue in this play), the fairies must fix their mistake. By act 3, scene 2, *both* men are enamored of Helena, and neither loves Hermia. Helena is furious, believing the men are mocking her; Hermia—*also* furious—believes Helena has willfully stolen Lysander from her. And the young men are ready to fight for Helena's love.

The scene is befuddling—and the lovers indistinguishable—in a way that insinuates the disorientation of *all* longing, the loss of identity in being-pulled-elsewhere than where we are. Shakespeare's parody of longing and pursuit reaches its peak as Oberon asks Puck, who's delighting in the confusion he's caused ("Lord, what fools these mortals be!"), to "overcast the night" with fog until the would-be combatants collapse in exhaustion. Helena then enters, laments the "weary night," and lies down to sleep. She's followed by Hermia, who, "never so weary, never so in woe," speaks this line: "My legs can keep no pace with my desires." Then she, too, lies down and sleeps.

If you've seen the play in performance, you may have sensed both the imminent reconciliation and the quiet onstage pause of slumber at this point—a suspension of the desiring mind-chatter that's prompted the lovers' every action thus far. If I were in the director's chair, I'd stretch this sleep scene out, so the whole of the theater could experience a reprieve from all the keeping-pace, the pursuing-of-the-other, that the lovers have done until now. The phrase "keep pace" had emerged in the decades before Shakespeare wrote *Midsummer*; it meant "to maintain the same speed" or "advance at an equal rate." But if we know anything about desire (and, oh, we know it as well as Hermia does), we know there *is* no keeping pace with craving. There's no stretching out wide enough (*pace* comes from *pandere*: "to stretch or extend, as in a stride") to keep up with our wanting. And our attempts to "stretch" ourselves toward what we desire only end up contorting us—distorting our sense of who we are, *as* we are, without them.

Through Lear and Richard, we examined *dukkha dukkha,* the suffering that arises in response to unpleasant experiences—birth and death, respectively. *Vipariṇāma dukkha,* on the other hand, is the suffering that arises in response to the loss of *pleasant* ones. It's occasioned by impermanence (*vipariṇāma* means "change"): namely, when the things we're fond of slip through our hands—which they always do, sooner or later. We experience *vipariṇāma dukkha* when we want what's impermanent to be permanent, which is tantamount to wanting it to be other than what it is. Naturally, this will always disappoint us.

Because there's no pleasurable experience that's enduring, there's no pleasurable experience that's perfectly satisfying. And if we're paying attention, we might notice a pinch of discomfort or unease *even in the midst of* our most pleasant experiences, because we have an acute awareness of the imminent nonexistence of our present joy. In that consciousness of the gap between now and later, even our most delightful experiences are tinged as they occur. It's a different kind of anguish than pain, to be sure: a subtle ache we might hardly discern. To observe the Noble Truth of *dukkha* when you're sick is one thing, but to see the suffering in joy is to see the sweeping truth of *dukkha* in an unawakened life.

I find Hermia—and her failing legs, and her too-fast desires—to be a fascinating example of *vipariṇāma dukkha* on the heels of separation from the beloved. She was beloved of two men, and then she was beloved of *none*. The origin of her suffering is impermanence: the end of being-loved by Lysander. But Hermia's admission that she "cannot keep pace" also points to what the Buddha described as the ongoing dissatisfaction inherent in a life of unawakened perspective: *not* getting what we want and being given what we *don't* want. Indeed, Hermia experiences both forms of *dukkha* in this play—running *away* from Demetrius, running *after* Lysander. These are sprints that might feel profoundly familiar.

That Hermia collapses from fatigue after delivering this line is worth lingering on. What are we exhausting in our longing? What vitality are we expending that could be used elsewhere in trying to "keep pace" with our craving, to "stretch out" our legs and prolong our pleasant experiences? In our desire to lengthen a moment we *lose* it for failing to have been *in* it, or for only having had one leg in all along. If we can observe those quiet sensations of dissatisfaction in the midst of joy, that's an invitation to honor the delicious impermanence of the present, palms open, ungraspingly. Honoring the transience of all that's exquisite but isn't ours (which is *everything*) allows for deeper presence, because we're not withdrawing from the moment to ponder how to *keep* it. What's more, we'll maintain our unstretched shapes by finding contentment in our present-tense forms—the ones that aren't distorting themselves to run *from* or run *to*, but have both feet fully in this wildly precious *now*.

THE SUFFERING OF CONDITIONED REALITY: HAMLET'S DUST

What a piece of work is a man! How noble in reason, how infinite in faculty, in form and moving how express and admirable, in action how like an angel, in apprehension how like a god—the beauty of the world, the paragon of animals! And yet to me what is this quintessence of dust?

—*HAMLET*, ACT 2, SCENE 2

amlet portrays the passage into madness—whether real or feigned is a matter of endless conjecture—of a prince who's visited by his father's ghost and told his uncle was his father's murderer. Hamlet vows to avenge his father's life and puts "an antic [bizarre] disposition on" while he determines his best course of action. Ultimately, *in*action is Hamlet's tragic flaw. But as he tarries, the play's other characters have time to concoct their own theories for the prince's "distemper": King Hamlet's death, his widowed queen's "o'erhasty marriage," Hamlet's love of Ophelia and her rejection of his advances. To discover the *true* source of Hamlet's erratic behavior, his mother and uncle summon his university companions, Rosencrantz and Guildenstern, to Elsinore. The royal couple's hope is that the scholars can cheer Hamlet out of his melancholy, or at the very least, discover its cause.

But while Hamlet is initially delighted to see his "ex'llent good friends" at court, it doesn't take him long to perceive what's going on. The scholars dodge the question of what brought them to this "prison," so Hamlet promises to save them the effort of spying by explicitly revealing why they were summoned. (I often imagine both characters naively leaning in at this moment, in expectation of something sensational.) Wanting only to toy with his deceitful friends now, the prince enters into a grandiloquent speech that ultimately tells them nothing more than what they already knew: *he's rather sad.* The "most excellent canopy" of the sky, Hamlet declares, "this majestical roof fretted with golden fire—why, it appears no other thing to me than a foul and pestilent congregation of vapours." It seems the prince can't see the stars for the immoral fog of humankind. And understandably so. Elsinore is a world of social advancement, of duplicity, of persons-as-pawns. Rosencrantz and Guildenstern are two of them.

Hamlet's friends and *Hamlet's* audience are offered a glimpse of inexhaustible beauty and potential in the above lines before Hamlet demolishes that grandeur before our very eyes. Humankind is a work of art, boundless in powers of thought and understanding, remarkable in form. But it's *also* only a "quintessence of dust." *Quintessence* means "fifth essence" (after earth, air, fire, and water). In ancient philosophy and medieval alchemy, it referred to ether: the substance of which the stars and planets were composed, and the most perfect or precious part latent in all things. Unlike the four earthly elements that composed matter, quintessence was believed to be incorruptible, incapable of change or decay. So Hamlet's "quintessence of dust" is a contradiction in terms— *the incorruptible corrupted, the eternal temporary* ("dust" is what matter decays to). There's also some sense in this speech that "quintessence" is, paradoxically, the very "foul and pestilent" star matter that's *clouding* Hamlet's sky. He can't perceive the heavens for all the heavenly dust in his way.

The third of the *dukkhas—saṅkhāra dukkha—*is the most subtle of the three sufferings; it's described as the suffering of conditioned existence. You might think of it as "background suffering": that nagging sensation that something isn't *quite* right in the undercurrents of our day-to-day existence. For some, *saṅkhāra dukkha* has its roots in impermanence—our underlying awareness that all of this is temporary, a substanceless puppet show that *is* becoming dust. For others, it's precipitated by the ongoing maintenance of staying alive—whether literally surviving or metaphorically upholding the illusion that there's a substantial self *at all*. For others still, *saṅkhāra dukkha* arises from a profound sense of separation from the phenomena of this world, that it's in our nature to experience attraction and aversion to those phenomena as they arise, or from our fruitless search for ultimate meanings and final truths. For some, it's the "prison" of the body in our own personal Denmarks—or, as Rosencrantz suggests to Hamlet, that this phenomenal world is simply "too narrow for our minds."

The irony of *saṅkhāra dukkha* is that it's a profound sense of the unsatisfactoriness of existence whose root cause is *unawakened* existence. This is the gorgeous tension Hamlet points to in these lines. Man's "reason" and "faculty," "form" and "apprehension" are nothing short of miraculous. But—like stars that obstruct the stars—it's precisely these elements of humanness that can obscure us from ourselves, that can lead us to believe we're nothing *but* faculty or form if we let them. Reason and faculty, form and apprehension will ultimately dissatisfy us if we think they're all there *is*.

Buddhists don't believe in an incorruptible quintessence: that clashes with the idea of *anatta*, non-self. But Buddhism *does* contain a core teaching that resembles a definition of quintessence given above: the most perfect or precious part latent in all things. Mahāyāna traditions call this principle Buddha Nature (*tathāgatagharba*: "Buddha womb," the indwelling of the Buddha). Theravādin traditions call it Luminous Mind (*pabhassara citta*): the perfected nature and potentiality for enlightenment that's innate in all sentient beings. Its central idea is that the fundamental nature of our mind *is* wisdom and compassion, and its origin can be traced back to the Buddha's words as recorded in the Pabhassara Sutta: "Luminous, monks, is the mind. And it is defiled by incoming defilements.

The uninstructed . . . person doesn't discern that . . . [it] is present."[31] In other words, Luminous Mind is *right here*, whether or not we're aware of it. And just as Hamlet can't see the stars for the "vapours" of dishonest humanity and conditioned existence, the metaphor in Buddhism is one of light *interrupted*. Buddha Nature and Luminous Mind are the sun obscured by clouds of attachment, delusion, defilements—though they're always shining brilliantly just behind them.

To uncover the sky—to glimpse the heavens beyond our dust—we simply stay still and awake to whatever is here. We watch the defilements (greed, anger, arrogance, complacency) arise and take shape as temporary phenomena (thoughts, feelings, sensations, perceptions, opinions). And then we watch them go, as they will, without interfering or identifying with them. In time, what's at first only glimpsed as flashes of space between dust-and-vapor thoughts is perceived as exceeding spaciousness. The gaps between mental phenomena become more expansive as we stop believing or relying on them when they arise—because experience tells us their essential nature is to release. That gap, that spaciousness, is the awareness of our Buddha Nature.

Hamlet's world is indeed clouded over with the fog of *saṅkhāra dukkha*—the feeling that "something is rotten in the state of Denmark," though no one can quite put their finger on it. Buddhism might suggest it's a "vapour" that prevents the prince from seeing that humankind is even *more* boundless

----

31 "Pabhassara Sutta: Luminous," AN 1.49–52. Access to Insight, last modified November 30, 2013, http://www.accesstoinsight.org/tipitaka/an/an01/an01.049.than.html.

and wondrous than he expresses here, and that the suffering of conditioned existence can be worked with. (*Rot*, after all, is part of a natural cycle of decay and regeneration, life created from death.) As the great thirteenth- and fourteenth-century Tibetan master Rangjung Dorjé, the Third Karmapa, wrote in his "Treatise on Buddha Nature": "All beings are Buddhas, but obscured by incidental stains. When those have been removed, there is Buddhahood."[32]

....

32 Quoted by the Venerable Khenchen Thrangu Rinpoche, in *Instructions on Treatise entitled: A Teaching on the Essence of the Tathagatas (The Tathagatagarbha)' by the Third Gyalwa Karmapa, Rangjung Dorje, according to An Illumination of the Thoughts of Rangjung Dorje: A Commentary to 'The Treatise that Teaches the Buddha Nature' by Jamgon Kongtrul Lodrö Thaye the Great.* Translated by Peter Roberts. Accessed on August 13, 2021, http://www.dharmadownload.net/pages/english/Natsok/0010_Teaching_English/Teaching_English_0035.htm.

NON-SELF AND PROSPERO'S PAUSED ART

Lie there, my art.

—*THE TEMPEST*, ACT 1, SCENE 2

The magician at the heart of *The Tempest* has already taught us something about impermanence, but we're not quite done with him—or he with *us*. It's in this scene that we discover Prospero's powers and the degree to which he's manipulating the very play we're witnessing. He's just orchestrated a storm to shipwreck his brother, who overthrew him as Duke of Milan twelve years ago. Once Antonio is ashore, the magician will arrange his brother's punishment and—depending on how aligned you think Prospero's conduct is with his claim that "the rarer action is / In virtue than in vengeance"— his redemption. Prospero's daughter Miranda has watched the ship sink from shore; assuming the storm is her father's doing, she asks him to "allay" the sea. Prospero assures her he's caused "no harm" to anyone aboard. But the time is ripe for Miranda, who "art ignorant of what thou art," to know her history. The father asks his daughter to help "pluck my magic garment from me" and tenderly addresses the cloak as he lays it on the ground: "Lie there, my art." With his grip on his "art" temporarily loosened, the family narrative can begin.

Much has been written about how Prospero's magic powers correspond to the powers of the playwright, who conceives and controls entire worlds. As is often the case with world-making, Prospero's ego is *the point*: his sorcery affords him a "look what I can do" attitude that culminates in the supernatural masque he produces for Miranda's betrothal that we saw in the chapter, and meditation, on *annica*. *The Tempest* is a series of power displays that reinforce Prospero's identity—an identity he's toiled for, as the history he now tells Miranda attests: once "rapt in secret studies," Prospero "neglect[ed] worldly ends" to dedicate himself to mastery in magic. But as Prospero sets his cloak down, he appears willing to unfasten himself from the identity he labored so diligently to create—at least while he rehearses its creation.

The more familiar definition of *art* is skill obtained through study or practice; but by the late sixteenth century, it had also begun to mean "skill in cunning and trickery," deception. Prospero's cloak, which he lays down in the stage directions, refers not only to a garment, but also to something that conceals or obscures. (Some editions of *The Tempest* call Prospero's garment a "mantle" instead; but wonderfully, the wordplay is still operative. A mantle is a loose, sleeveless cloak; as a verb it means "to disguise or conceal.") Add to this the multivalence in the word *lie*: "to place in a recumbent position; to speak falsely (of)." In short, there's a *lot* of deception nestled in both this line and the stage direction that precedes it. One of my favorite glosses of Prospero's "lie there" observes that "Lord Burleigh, when he put off his gown at night, used to say 'Lie there, Lord Treasurer.'"[33] Shakespeare may have been playing on the nightly practice of Queen Elizabeth's chief advisor here. Burleigh and Prospero both mark a distinction between who they *are* and the roles they play, the costumes they put on that shroud them. Or, at the very least, they suspect that their robes—and by extension, their titles—are not what *make* them. What a familiar weight, indeed, to take off one's shoulders at the end of every day.

Among the more notable quotes misattributed to the Buddha is that "there is no self." Buddhist scriptures tell us otherwise. When the Buddha is asked point-blank in the Ānanda Sūtta "Is there a self?" he remains silent. When the question is then posed from the other side—"Then is there *no* self?"—the Buddha *also* declines to answer.[34] It's a resounding silence, and it implies that the question itself is an obstacle on the path to awakening. Yet the misattribution has probably survived because it superficially resembles the Buddhist teaching on *anatta*—*not*-self or *non*-self, rather than *no* self.

The Vedic teachings of the Buddha's day maintained that within each of us is an eternal and unchanging soul (Sanskrit:

<hr />

33 John Ford, *The Dramatic Works of John Ford*, vol. 1 (New York: J. and J. Harper, 1831), 58.

34 "Ananda Sutta: To Ananda," SN 44.10, Access to Insight, last modified November 30, 2013, http://www.accesstoinsight.org/tipitaka/sn/sn44/sn44.010.than.html.

ātman). Buddhism's *anatta*, on the other hand, proposes that there *is* no permanent, enduring essence. *Anatta* is the last of the three marks of phenomenal existence, which include impermanence (*anicca*) and suffering (*dukkha*). Of these marks, nonself is the characteristic that probably conforms least to our lived experience. After all, here we are, having entered a form. *My* form looks different than *yours* does. It has its own hands, its own head, its own heart, its own volition. It's lived a set of life experiences yours has not; and it perceives that sequence of experiences as its own personal continuity, its history. It looks out at *your* form, your being-in-the-world; and it can't know where you came from or imagine what you're thinking or how it feels for your body to walk, or to sit, or to see, or to breathe. Its experiences have evolved into patterns: desires, thoughts, and actions that it calls, collectively, "I." And of course this whole process feels absolutely natural to it. Because it is a *person*, a *persona*—a word that refers to the mask worn by an actor, the part that one plays in a drama.

Yet when we hold the notion of a permanent, unchanging "self," a special entity we identify with, we want to give it priority. And to the extent that we identify with it, we spend our lives protecting it; defending it; scrambling to justify it; fearing its insufficiency, or its failure, or its loss. Identity evokes corollary feelings of pride, clinging, jealousy, ill will, and fear. And it's ultimately self-bondage, because we make decisions based on what will verify our stories of self, rather than recognizing the ever-changing, wide-open field of interbeing, in which we're constantly in relation with others. This narrow, reified sense of self produces a competition of interests and counterinvestments between beings whose lives and interests are actually deeply, inextricably interdependent. And we miss out on experiences of benevolence, of sympathetic joy (*mudita*), of reciprocal encouragement, of intimacy. All because we refuse to take the mask off and to put the mantle down.

Buddhism's non-self is a strategy for disassembling our notion of a unified entity and dispensing with all the unskillful work we do to uphold it. (Magic, after all, is manipulation.) As such, the teaching of *anatta* is an answer *not* to the question "Is there a self?" but to the question of how we might lessen our suffering and the suffering of those around us. I love that Prospero describes Miranda as "ignorant of what thou art." "Being" and "deception" merge in that final word. Prospero ultimately resumes his mantle and carries on with his revenge, because as soon as he's reidentified with "self," revenge *matters*. But the phrase "Lie there, my art" is worth taking up whenever we find ourselves identifying with something inconstant, something non-self. Perhaps we metaphorically—even tenderly, as Prospero does—put that thing down for a moment, let it "lie" on the wisdom-drenched earth long enough to watch it transform. Perhaps we tell the story of our magic cloak aloud, listening for the parts of the narrative we're uncompromising about, how those parts start to yield, even as we observe their insistence. And *then* we can "assume the mantle" once again with some playfulness, because—as with everything in this phenomenal existence—we know it is not enduring.

The Three
Unwholesome
Roots

"TO GUARD A THING NOT OURS": GREED IN *TROILUS AND CRESSIDA*

. . . we have lost so many tenths of ours
To guard a thing not ours . . .

—*TROILUS AND CRESSIDA*, ACT 2, SCENE 2

Troilus and Cressida places us in the midst of the Trojan War—a war that erupted when a Trojan prince named Paris abducted Helen, wife of the Greek Menelaus and the most beautiful woman in the world. We're now seven years into the war and at a stalemate, the Greek army encamped outside the walls of Troy. *Within* those walls, King Priam—Paris's and Hector's father—and his men are conferring about a peace proposal extended by the Greeks: they'll withdraw from Troy and end the conflict if Paris will only return Helen. Priam turns to Hector first for his judgment. The eldest son, and Troy's best warrior, advocates for Helen's return: she's not worth the price Troy is paying to keep her. Every Trojan ("every tithe-soul") that's been killed in this war, Hector argues, was as valuable as Helen. And if persons have analogous value, Helen's *single* life is hardly commensurate with the thousands of lives her possession has cost them. Add to this the element of (non-) ownership. "If we have lost so many tenths of ours / To guard a thing not ours," then reason recommends we surrender her.

It's an argument that confirms Hector as one of *Troilus and Cressida*'s nobler characters—a fairly simple feat in a play in which the great figures of Greek myth are otherwise reduced to folly. Shakespeare's sources for the play include Homer's *Iliad* and Chaucer's *Troilus and Criseyde*—epic poems in which Hector figures as the ideal warrior and leader of Troy's forces. A perceptive reader feels the playwright constrained by the mythic figure as he makes Hector the lone voice of reason *and* allows him to eventually capitulate. (The war must go on, after all, as it does in the legend.) So while Hector initially argues that Helen is "not worth what she doth cost / The holding," he soon concedes to Troilus, who argues for "manhood and honour," "glory," "renown," and "fame." While Hector might not be persuaded by *Helen's* worth, he's certainly seduced by the theme of *his own*. And so: three more years of war. And Troy's loss. And Hector's pitiful death.

Rāga (attachment, greed, desire) is one of the Three Poisons or Three Unwholesome Roots (*akusala mūla*), along with *dosa* (aversion, hate) and *moha* (delusion). You might think of *rāga*, *dosa*, and *moha* as variations on the themes "I like," "I *don't* like," and "I don't *care.*" They're understood as by-products of igno-rance, the root of all other *kilesas* (unwholesome states of mind that manifest in unwholesome actions), and the fundamental reason we're unhappy rather than merrily enlivened by life. *Rāga* is defined as any form of attachment to a sensory object or to the pleasure derived from objects of the senses. *The Path of Purification (Visuddhimagga)*, one of the most important treatises of Theravāda Buddhism, says of *rāga* that "its proxi-mate cause is seeing enjoyment in things that lead to bondage."[35] What enables *rāga* to function is actually a misattribution of source: we believe external objects, *rather than the mind that perceives or interacts with them*, "give" us pleasure. The good news? If pleasure is of the mind, then it's always already *here.* It requires only a re-vision of source to connect with it.

We probably need only a few moments of honest introspec-tion to observe the ways *rāga* shows up in our lives. It arises each time we confuse the biological need to preserve and pro-tect ourselves with a desire for nonessential needs—things that ensure the survival of the *ego* rather than of the biological body. It's present each time we turn to anything outside ourselves, yearning for the satisfaction or fulfillment or contentment we think it will bring: objects, experiences, titles, relationships, recognition, money, or—in the Trojans' case—glory. Some-times it manifests as a desire to *feel* a certain way, or to *keep* feeling a certain way. Because as often as *rāga* looks like a state of lack, it also arises from the longing to *continue* possessing the

---

35 Bhadantācariya Buddhaghosa, *The Path of Purification (Visuddhimagga)*, trans. Bhikkhu Ñāṇamoli (Kandy: Buddhist Publication Society, 2011), 476.

various "Helens" we suppose we already possess. Sometimes we erroneously call this need to safeguard "love"; often it feels more like fear. Because whether we've wed these objects of the senses or abducted them, they are fleeting, ephemeral, impermanent. Yet we try desperately to "guard things not ours"— things, indeed, that never were ours in the first place.

Buddhism says that's worth reflecting on. It's an invitation to ask ourselves what we're ultimately after, *what* to seek and where to seek it, if we truly want happiness. The Buddha offered antidotes—alternative mental states—for each of the Three Unwholesome Roots. The antidote to *rāga* is *dāna*: generosity, contentment, detachment, selflessness. *Dāna* takes many forms, though traditionally Buddhists speak of four types of giving: giving material aid, giving teachings and advice, providing protection from fear, and giving love. However obvious, these are all forms of offering, unclenching our anyhow-futile grip on the things of this world, letting them be-for-all—and letting them simply *be*. Thubten Chodron tells a wonderful story about an old woman in the Buddha's time who was extremely miserly. The Buddha gave her a carrot and a very simple practice to accompany it: have her right hand give the carrot to her left hand, and her left hand give it back. "Try it some time," Chodron advises:

> Sit there and give it from one hand to the other hand; then at one point imagine that the hand you give it to is attached to somebody else's body. Why is there a difference? Why is it that passing the carrot from one of my own hands to the other is okay, but if it's attached

to somebody else's body I feel lost? A hand is still a
hand. Really do it sometime, and look at your hands
and think about this.[36]

At one point in the Trojan conference, Troilus exclaims,
"O theft most base, / that we have stol'n what we do fear to
keep!" It's an outburst meant to justify continued warfare, but
the word *theft* is worth lingering on as it relates to *rāga*, which
is always a greed for what was never ours. The fear Troilus calls
attention to, alongside the "lost tenths" and "tithe-souls" Hector grieves, are a consequence of the wasted labor of defending "having." We lose no small portion of ourselves in gripping
what's bound to slip right through our hands—whether it's a
carrot, or a relationship, or a title, or a thought. Indeed, we lose
a *holy fraction* (Hector's "tenth" and "tithe" converge in the idea
of what is due to the divine). We miss out on the sacredness of
what *is*, the radical blessing of here-and-now. Of all the por-
tions Shakespeare could've chosen to put in Hector's mouth at
this moment, "losing a tenth" carries remarkable significance.
May we not, in our desire to grasp and guard, forget that these
fractions of our lives can instead be a holy offering—*dāna*—to
all beings, including ourselves. And the most precious tithe we
can give ourselves is the gift of wanting only what's here, for
exactly as long as it's with us.

....

36 Thubten Chodron, "The Three Forms of Generosity," accessed August 14, 2021,
https://thubtenchodron.org/1993/11/giving-material-aid-freedom-from-fear-dharma/.

"I SUP UPON MYSELF":
SELF-CONSUMING ANGER
IN *CORIOLANUS*

Anger's my meat, I sup upon myself,
And so shall starve with feeding.

—*CORIOLANUS*, ACT 4, SCENE 2

Volumnia is the mother of the great Roman general Caius Martius, who's inherited both her valiance and her pride. She thrust her son off to war "when yet he was but tenderbodied." She keeps a running tally of his war scars. She lives vicariously through his heroism yet rules him through reminders that "thy valiantness was mine; thou sucked'st it from me." And when Caius Martius receives a hero's welcome after nearly single-handedly defeating a neighboring tribe in the city of Corioli—earning the name Coriolanus—she compels him to accept the consulship the Senate nominates him for. But there's a catch: elected officials are expected to show public displays of humility by seeking the citizens' votes in the marketplace. And Coriolanus—wholly his mother's son—abhors the common people. The marketplace scene is remarkable for the ways Coriolanus visibly recoils *even as* he seeks the commoner's "voices" for his mother's sake. Two Roman tribunes, Brutus and Sicinius, call attention to the scorn in his performance. Incited by the tribunes, the people banish Coriolanus from Rome—the city he's struck so many "noble blows" for.

You can imagine what this does to his characteristically volatile mother. Volumnia discharges her rage upon the tribunes when she meets them next. When the assault is over, Menenius—Coriolanus's friend and father figure, who was present for the encounter—praises Volumnia for having "told them home" and asks if she'll dine with him. But even after her passionate outburst, Volumnia's fury persists. "Anger's my meat" is her response to the invitation. "I sup upon myself, / And so shall starve with feeding." *I'm too enraged to consume anything but myself.*

It's an RSVP of misconceived grief and a remarkable metaphor—one made even more remarkable by the fact that the play's backdrop is a famine in Rome: the commoners are *literally* starving behind Volumnia's metaphor of malnutrition. Feeding-to-starvation is an idea Shakespeare savored; you'll find it again in *Antony and Cleopatra* (Cleopatra "makes hungry / Where she most satisfies") and *Pericles* (Juno "starves the ears she feeds, and makes them hungry"). The difference is that *Volumnia's* consumption is cannibalistic: she's the object of her own digestion. And the metaphor isn't only self-destructive; it's also non-nutritive. Volumnia is consuming a "meat" that's angry—indeed, that is anger itself. It's a toxic cycle of engorgement and starvation that, one imagines, eventually leaves nothing but an angry mouth—a hole with nothing left to devour.

Anger (*dosa*, also translated as "hatred" or "aversion") is the second of Buddhism's Three Unwholesome Roots—detrimental mental states that cloud the mind and produce unwholesome action. Whereas *rāga* is a variation on "I want," *dosa* is a variation on "I *don't* want." Anger and hatred are often identified as the most destructive of the *kilesas* because of how easily they degenerate into violence and aggression, instantly incinerating whole forests of positive merit we've worked to create. Shantideva, the eighth-century Buddhist scholar who wrote *A Guide to the Bodhisattva's Way of Life* (*Bodhicaryāvatāra*), maintained that "there is no evil like hatred."[37] "Conquer anger with non-anger; conquer wickedness with goodness," says the Buddha in *The Dhammapada*.[38]

As we undertake the luminous journey of engaging with this fierce world, we're bound to come into direct relationship with powerful emotions that can easily lead to outrage. The raw energy of these emotions is neither "good" nor "bad"; but it can be *reacted* to unskillfully (violence, suppression) or harnessed and transformed skillfully. Buddhist teachings tell

....

37 Acharya Shantideva, *A Guide to the Bodhisattva's Way of Life*, trans. Stephen Batchelor (Dharamsala: Library of Tibetan Works and Archives, 1979), p. 56, https://www.tibethouse.jp/about/buddhism/text/pdfs/Bodhisattvas_way_English.pdf.
38 Gil Fronsdal, *The Dhammapada* (Boston: Shambhala, 2005), 55.

us that the antidotes to anger are loving-kindness, patience, and compassion. When Shantideva said "there is no evil like hatred," he didn't leave it at that. He followed it with: "[there is no] fortitude like patience."[39] We experience anger and hatred because we actually feel something *deeper* than them: fear, embarrassment, shame, anxiety, helplessness, or—like Volumnia—profound grief. Anger and hatred are reactive strategies that *appear* to give us control through aggression—though that's precisely what escalates the suffering. Still, our deeper vulnerability is more difficult to look at; so we opt for hardening, for closing down. And when we're alone in an enclosed system, the self-consumption begins.

This is where Shantideva's patience comes in. Buddhist teacher Pema Chödrön tenderly reminds us that "initially there is some softness" in the pain that precedes anger. "If you're fast, you can catch it," she writes; but usually we "don't even realize there is any softness" before we reactively go hard.[40] Patience and loving-kindness ask us to sit quietly until that initial, reactive hardness dissolves, to find the softness *within* the noisy, hot energy of anger and connect with it. Experiencing the anger, investigating its nature, is a form of slow, wholesome digestion. It listens and looks for what's beneath the outrage. It transforms our subsurface observations into clarity, mirror-like wisdom, energy for action. And because patience makes us soft rather

39 Acharya Shantideva, *A Guide to the Bodhisattva's Way of Life,* trans. Stephen Batchelor (Dharamsala: Library of Tibetan Works and Archives, 1979), p. 56, https://www.tibethouse.jp/about/buddhism/text/pdfs/Bodhisattvas_way_English.pdf.
40 Pema Chödrön, "The Answer to Anger and Aggression Is Patience," Lion's Roar, accessed August 4, 2021, https://www.lionsroar.com/the-answer-to-anger-aggression-is-patience/.

than hard, open rather than shut, we're no longer self-enclosed and self-consuming.

Touching into the vulnerability beneath anger and hatred breaks us open, keeps us from eating ourselves. When we take the time to watch anger go soft, we remember that it, like all emotions, is transitory. And because we no longer understand it as *our* anger, we're no longer "supping upon ourselves." None of this, of course, is to discount the pain of having one's only son banished—or whatever the pain of your moment is. But it places us on the threshold of something *other* than aversion and aggression. At that threshold we are throbbing with the possibility of an awakened self-compassion that sparks loving compassion for others. "You may feel that you're going to die, or that something is going to die," Pema Chödrön writes of the patience and willingness-to-look that's required to keep us from self-consuming. "And you will be right . . . something will die. But it's something that needs to die and you will benefit greatly from its death."[41]

This is such a different death than Volumnia's eating herself into nothingness. It's a death that makes one more living.

---

[41] Chödrön, "The Answer."

WANDERING IN ILLUSIONS IN
THE COMEDY OF ERRORS

And here we wander in illusions.

—*THE COMEDY OF ERRORS*, ACT 4, SCENE 3

Antipholus of Syracuse is standing bewildered in the street in the midst of a play whose plot is propelled by mistaken identity. Over twenty years ago, two sets of identical twins—Antipholus among them—were separated in a shipwreck. Two boys landed in Ephesus, the other two in Syracuse with Egeon, who renamed them after their lost (and presumed-dead) brothers. It's a decision that dissolves the only distinctions between the twins. And it ultimately disorients *everyone* when the Syracusan pair goes traveling one day, and the four men—twins going by the same names as their brothers—find themselves in the same city.

Antipholus of *Ephesus* is a wealthy and well-loved merchant in town, and his prominence only exacerbates the confusion that follows. The citizens hand money to his newly arrived Syracusan twin; they extend him all manner of invitations. A gold chain his brother ordered has just been delivered to *him* instead. But the bountiful goods and lavish treatment he's receiving aren't worth the price of his bewilderment. Without an explanation for how the citizens know them by name, the Syracusans determine that Ephesus is possessed by "dark-working sorcerers" and "soul-killing witches," and they must leave. "I will not harbour in this town tonight," determines Antipholus—a decision that's confirmed when his slave Dromio enters with bail to free the *other* Antipholus from jail. (Naturally, the merchant twin refused to pay for a gold chain he never received, and was arrested for it.) "The fellow is distraught," Antipholus of Syracuse says of Dromio, "and so am I, / And here we wander in illusions."

Each time I picture Antipholus of Syracuse speaking these lines, the gold chain he's wearing that doesn't belong to him glistens sharply beneath the stage lights as he articulates the word *illusion*. (In my vision, the chain is always comically large.) *Illusion* comes from *illudere*—"to play with"—and it originally meant scorning, derision, or mockery. Over time it came to be associated with sensory confusion: being deceived by appearances, the attribution of reality to what is *un*real. As though someone were playing with the very fabric of the world as Antipholus knows it.

"As Antipholus knows it" is the key phrase there. According to Buddhism, Antipholus's predicament in this scene is familiar to all of us. And no one needs to mistake our identities for us to experience it, because we're already mistaking *ourselves*.

The Pāli word *moha* means delusion, confusion, or wrong view; it's the last of the Three Unwholesome Roots we've been examining. In the Sūtta on the Adherents of Other Faiths (Aññatitthiya Sūtta), the Buddha explains that *rāga* arises "for one who attends improperly to a beautiful object," *dosa* "for one who attends improperly to a repulsive object," and *moha* "for one who attends improperly to *things*."[42] "Things" might feel like a remarkably broad category, the possibilities a little too vast to put a finger on. And while greed and hatred are louder and easier to recognize, we can live our entire lives with *moha* flying under our radar. That's because *moha* deals in "the world as we know it"—the world as it seems experientially obvious to us when we're not attending to things as they *are*. Or rather, when we're too distracted by the world, at its surface, to see it for what it is.

As vipassana meditation teacher S. N. Goenka describes it, those in *moha* "take untruth as truth, [and] what is insubstantial as substantial. . . . So long as one regards what is impermanent as permanent, suffering as happiness, and no[n]-self as self, one will be strongly fettered by *moha*."[43] This is, you'll notice, where *moha* meets the Three Marks of Existence: impermanence, suffering, non-self. When we "miss the Marks," so to speak, that's where *moha* finds us.

The antidote to *moha* is *paññā*, wisdom. It entails a willingness to sincerely and critically examine our most deeply held beliefs about "the world as we know it." Often it entails

42 "Aññatitthiya Sutta," Buddhist Publication Society, accessed August 4, 2021, http://www.buddha-vacana.org/sutta/anguttara/03/an03-069.html.
43 S. N. Goenka, "What Exactly Does 'Moha' Mean?" Vipassana Research Institute, accessed August 4, 2020, https://www.vridhamma.org/node/2151.

uncovering what those beliefs even *are*, because we've confused them all along with what we've casually called "reality." So we must dig in even—and perhaps especially—to what we've considered self-evident truths. *Paññā* is an invitation to distinguish the stories we hold from what's unchanging *beneath* those stories. It demands an open heart, a beginner's mind, a willingness to be astonished—and perhaps disoriented—as we're dislodged from our delusion into true knowing. (Perhaps the names we have *now*, for example—like two of the *Comedy*'s twins—are *not* the names we've had forever.)

The moment after Antipholus of Syracuse observes that he's "wandering in illusions," a courtesan enters and asks him to return the ring she'd given his twin brother at dinner. Master and slave—still believing Ephesus enchanted—are certain she's "the devil's dam" in women's clothing. "It is written," Dromio cautions, that such beings "appear to men like angels of light. Light is an effect of fire, and fire will burn." It's a biblical warning to his master not to come too near the courtesan. But it also happens to echo the Buddha's metaphor of delusion as fire. The Buddha first introduced the Three Unwholesome Roots in his Fire Sermon (Ādittapariyāya Sūtta), in which he declares: "All is burning . . . burning with what? Burning with the fire of lust, with the fire of hate, with the fire of delusion."[44] The word *nirvana* (Pāli: *nibbāna*) literally means "blowing out" or "quenching," the putting-out of a fire. Its simplest definition in Buddhism is the extinguishing of the Unwholesome Roots: *rāga*, *dosa*, and *moha*.

....
44 "Adittapariyaya Sutta: The Fire Sermon," SN 35.28, Access to Insight, last modified June 13, 2010, http://www.accesstoinsight.org/tipitaka/sn/sn35/sn35.028.nymo.html.

For those who are not yet awakened, the phenomenal world is on fire. (For *awakened* beings, on the other hand, everything that appears is the indivisible union of bliss and emptiness.) But although it's burning, it's the only world we *have* in which to do the work of awakening. As we live in it, we're distracted from the transcendent by the visible: the gold chains that impress themselves upon our senses, the calling of "our" names. *Paññā*—which begins with a receptiveness even to the *possibility* that we're wandering in illusion—is meant to liberate us from our clinging to the "facts" and facets of this world which is but a dream. What begins to shift for us when we take our most deeply held beliefs, turn them over tenderly in our wondering hands, and allow ourselves to sit with the delightful possibility that they, too, are illusions that can be extinguished?

The Four Noble Truths

MALVOLIO'S CELL AND THE DARKNESS OF IGNORANCE IN *TWELFTH NIGHT*

. . . there is no darkness but ignorance . . .

—*TWELFTH NIGHT*, ACT 4, SCENE 2

This line emerges from the literal darkness of a cell, in the voice of Feste the clown, who's disguised as a clergyman named Sir Topas. The "churchman" is speaking to Malvolio, steward to a rich countess named Olivia. Malvolio is the household puritan: bitterly serious, severe, with a narrow moral perspective and a will to *enforce* that perspective on everyone else, whose behavior he deplores and feels affronted by. The others see him as a contemptuous killjoy, and Olivia's riotous domestics decide to play a prank on him to expose his vanity and pretension. They forge a love letter—ostensibly from Olivia—cataloguing a series of ridiculous actions

Malvolio should perform if he wants to earn her favor and rise to "greatness." The list includes wearing yellow stockings: attire which would both offend puritan sensibilities and deviate from the livery he'd be expected to wear as a servant. His dreams of authority and rank within reach, Malvolio does all the forged letter bids him to. And so his humiliation comprises the subplot of the play.

If you've seen the play in performance, you know what a comic spectacle the yellow-stockinged scene can be. Malvolio's conduct is so contrary to his ordinary behavior that, knowing nothing of the fraudulent letter, Olivia believes he's gone mad ("Let this fellow be looked to," she charges her domestics). The others confine him to a dark chamber—a sixteenth-century cure for madness—where they can torment him further. This is why the clown is posed as a clergyman: to convince an imprisoned Malvolio that he truly *is* a "lunatic." (The costume change is unnecessary as it's dark in Malvolio's cell—"Thou mightst have done this without thy beard and gown," Maria says, "he sees thee not"—but it draws attention to the "art" of identity. Audiences would observe the contrast between the clergyman's dull robe and the clown's motley apparel beneath it as the scene unfolded.)

It's an amusing exchange if you can put aside your rising feelings of pity for Malvolio. Indeed, in the best performances of this play, audiences detest the steward until the cruelty of his confinement in this scene comes home to them. Malvolio tries desperately to enlist Sir Topas as an ally ("Do not think I am mad. They have laid me here in hideous darkness"), but Feste deflects his attempts to do so ("Sayst thou that house is dark? . . . Why, it hath bay windows transparent as barricadoes"). As the characters argue over what would seem an objective fact—Sir Topas contending Malvolio's claim that "this house is dark" is a sign of his madness—the clergyman-clown speaks this line: "Madman, thou errest. I say there is no darkness but ignorance."

The scene is an encounter of counterparts: the rigid puritan disputing with the man who lives by means of humor and wit; the character who perceives life in absolute terms being told things aren't *at all* as they appear by the figure—a jester, a fool—whose function is to jolt us out of our unbending perspectives. Malvolio's name means "ill will," but the "mal" also announces his mistaken view. Of course, Malvolio's in the dark in a few ways: literally, metaphorically (he knows nothing of the trick that's being played on him), and spiritually (he's blind to the world as it *is* because of how he thinks it *ought* to be).

The first of Buddhism's Four Noble Truths (*cattāri ariyasaccāni*) is that sentient beings experience suffering (*dukkha*)—a view we've covered at length. Its Second Noble Truth is that the cause of that suffering is craving (*taṇhā*) conditioned by ignorance (*avijjā*), or craving bound up in ignorance. In Pāli, the Second Noble Truth is referred to as *samudaya sacca*: "truth of the origin of suffering." It holds that ignorance is at the root of all our craving, and therefore, it's the only problem to be solved if we want to end our suffering. The craving that ignorance generates is of three kinds: (1) the craving for sensory pleasure (consider Malvolio's ambition to be

Olivia's lover), (2) the craving "to be" or "to become," which includes the craving to dominate others (consider Malvolio's desire to rule his fellow servants), and (3) the craving *not* to be, or to avoid what's unpleasant (consider Malvolio's desire to be released from his inferior social status). *Samudaya sacca* maintains that all three cravings arise from a fundamental misunderstanding of the nature of self and reality, which are ultimately impermanent and empty. So *who* is craving? And *why* would that one crave an ephemeral dream?

According to the Discourse on Right View (Sammādiṭṭhi Sūtta), "when a noble disciple has understood ignorance (*avijjā*), the origin of ignorance, the cessation of ignorance, and the way leading to the cessation of ignorance . . . [he] makes an end of suffering."[45] *Avijjā* is a negation; it means "not to see." Ask any Buddhist what those in *avijjā* "do not see," and you'll get a range of answers: the full meaning and implications of the Four Noble Truths, the law of *kamma* (cause and effect) or of interdependence, and so on. In Buddhist iconography, *avijjā* is often depicted as a blind or blindfolded man. The Chinese and Japanese symbols for *avijjā* show the character mu (無), a barrier or a negation, beside characters for the sun and moon (明), which represent wisdom and clarity. The walls of Malvolio's cell and the walls of his mind are like that mu: his ignorance is both literally and figuratively a state of darkness.

....

45 "Sammaditthi Sutta: The Discourse on Right View," MN 9, Access to Insight, last modified November 30, 2013, http://www.accesstoinsight.org/tipitaka/mn/mn.009.ntbb. html.

Buddhism suggests that eradicating ignorance can be as simple as ceasing to ignore, resolving to notice. It's recognizing our cravings—for *pleasure*, to *be*, or *not* to be (forgive the *Hamlet* pun)—and tracing them back to the blind beliefs that make them so. We witness when, like Malvolio, we're personally affronted when the world doesn't match our expectations of it. We see the jester's pants beneath the churchman's gown, the unreality of identity, the yellow stockings we don and the ways we "humiliate" (make-small) our vast selves for our worldly desires, how speedily those objects of desire dissolve. If we can see life as it *is*—and ourselves as we *are*—we'll conduct ourselves in ever-greater harmony with that seeing. That's where the light enters—sun, moon, and wisdom through the windows of our chambers. And then our chambers are no longer dark. And they're no longer chambers.

CANCELING CAPTIVITY AND FREEING THE PRISONER IN *JULIUS CAESAR*

So every bondman in his own hand bears
The power to cancel his captivity.

—*Julius Caesar*, ACT 1, SCENE 3

I t's been a day of unnatural omens in Rome. "Men all in fire walk[ed] up and down the streets"; lions trod the grounds near the Capitol; a "bird of night" shrieked above the marketplace at noon. Tonight, it's raging tempests: "all the sway of earth / Shakes like a thing unfirm," a breathless Casca remarks as the scene opens. Casca's been shaken by the day's bizarre occurrences. *Cassius*, on the other hand, has been baring his chest to the storm, reveling in it as a divine instrument of warning and of counsel. It's "a very pleasing night to honest men" he maintains against Casca's "fear and trembl[ing]." And so two figures of conflicting interpretation meet in the shadows of night, drenched and electrified in their own sensitivities.

Cassius has his own understanding of the day's events: *some-one*—"a man most like this dreadful night"—has become a bit too powerful for his own good. Knowing the name that Cassius won't speak, and uneasy since that withholding is keeping the men from a kind of conspiratorial intimacy, Casca comments that Caesar is soon to be crowned. It's enough to cause Cassius to pull out his dagger in a wild response to the prospect of tyranny. Neither "stony tower, nor walls of beaten brass, / Nor airless dungeon" can imprison him, Cassius claims. He'll "shake off" political oppression as he chooses. "So can I," Casca replies. "So every bondman in his own hand bears / The power to cancel his captivity." The metaphor is a gesture toward suicide: an inarticulate compact that the men will end their lives if the alternative is servitude to Caesar. Of course, if you know either the history or the play, you know their daggers ultimately "cancel" *elsewhere*, when they bury them in Caesar's body.

To *cancel* ("to cross out, draw a line through") is to nullify an obligation. The verb applies to two senses of the word *bond*, which Casca is playing on here: a deed constraining one to pay a sum of money to another (which gets crossed out in the document when annulled) and a slave. Both bonds bind, making one less free. But Casca's unfree body—the slave—takes metaphorical precedence here. *So every imprisoned man holds the tool to free himself in his own hand.* The figure of speech is a violent one, signaling release from the phenomenal world: *through our own cessation, we'll cease to be in thrall.* But from the point of view of spiritual practice, the lines become less about "last acts" that liberate the body and more about mental paradigm shifts that make-free our minds. In the line that precedes this, Cassius speaks of himself in the third person ("Cassius from bondage will deliver Cassius"), grammatically distancing himself from himself. It's through this remove, Buddhism proposes, that we release ourselves from our prisons.

Buddhism's first two Noble Truths are that suffering exists, and its origin is craving conditioned by ignorance. Its Third Noble Truth offers a solution to that suffering: the extinction of craving. *Nirodha*, etymologically related to the more familiar Sanskrit word *nirvana*, means "cessation of desire," "freedom from craving," "extinction of thirst." Sometimes it's simply translated as a "blowing out," as of a fire. But it's not an annihilation of self, because Buddhism says that there *isn't* one. *Nirodha* is the annihilation of the *illusion* of self—that there's even a "bondman" to *bind*—and of the cravings that accompany that illusion. As the Buddha states in his very first teaching, The Sūtta of the Wheel of Dhamma (Dhammacakkappavattana Sūtta): "This, monks, is the noble truth of the cessation of *dukkha*: the renunciation, relinquishment, release, and letting go of . . . craving."[46] *Nirodha* is experienced when one truly sees that all is impermanent, neither "me" nor "mine." And furthermore, that there's *no one* who is doing the realizing. *Nirodha is*, but the self who experiences *nirodha* is *not*.

....

46 "Dhammacakkappavattana Sutta: Setting the Wheel of Dhamma in Motion," SN 56.11, Access to Insight, last modified November 30 2013, http://www.accesstoinsight. org/tipitaka/sn/sn56/sn56.011.than.html.

There's an ancient Zen axiom that states "no self, no problem." Believing otherwise is to make bondmen of ourselves, trap ourselves in prisons of our own making. The metaphors in Eastern spiritual practices for "our captivity" vary. In some cases the prison door is locked but the prisoner holds the key; in others the door is closed but not locked; in still others the door stands wide open. In more complex metaphors we hang our keys on our cell walls, adorning the prisons we've become so intimate with and comfortable in. Or we become attached to a form *within* the prison—so focused on a spiritual practice that we miss how we're adding another brick to the walls with every repetition. Ultimately, the practice only reinforces our belief in a "self" who's "on the path toward liberation," that there's "one" who's becoming-free. In each of these cases—no matter the metaphor—Buddhism says that *there is no prisoner*, because no one is bound except by his believing mind. We *captive* ourselves by believing (in) our "selves." We *produce* the prison by ideating a key to "free" us.

One way of thinking about the captivity metaphor is that, in thinking we are selves, we become jailors and prisoners *both*. And yet, if we're both prisoner and jailor, we must *also* be the bricks that constitute the prison walls, Cassius's "stony tower," the trees and fields far beyond the prison grounds, the wind that rushes through them and the feathers on the birds that ruffle as it sings. We must be the lock and the key and the consciousness that comes up with both the incompetent and the ingenious-but-ineffectual escape plans. When we can realize this, we don't *need* to get up, walk to the door, and open it . . .

because we already *are* (the) outside. How, then, can there be a prisoner, let alone a door? And what, then, remains to crave?

Buddhism would tell Cassius and Casca that they've mistaken their daggers for keys, that one need not *leave* one's body to escape servitude to suffering. The key that "cancels captivity" is the vital recognition that we *are* it—and therefore, we are already liberated. To cancel is literally to cross something out. It's etymologically related to *carcer*, "prison." We *cancel* our *carcer* by drawing a line through the self. It's a liberating line that connects the prisoner, like a thread of interdependence, to everything else that *is*, and is *free*.

HAPPINESS BY VIRTUE ACHIEVED: *THE TAMING OF THE SHREW*

Virtue and that part of philosophy
Will I apply that treats of happiness
By virtue specially to be achieved.

—*The Taming of the Shrew*, ACT 1, SCENE 1

Lucentio and his servant Tranio have just arrived in Padua, "nursery of arts," where Lucentio intends to further his studies and "deck his fortune" with "virtuous deeds," ornamenting his social station with honorable action. I imagine the master's face aflush with the exhilaration of possibility as he announces his aim to Tranio in the above lines. But Shakespeare is setting us up to witness a well-intentioned objective turn short-lived. Lucentio's eagerness to "institute / A course of learning and ingenious studies" is promptly moderated by two matters: Tranio's appeal that they not neglect life's pleasures amid their academic pursuits ("while we do admire / This virtue and this moral discipline, / Let's be no stoics nor no stocks, I pray"); and the arrival of Bianca on the scene, whom Lucentio instantly falls in love with. This sharp swing—the displacement of devotion from scholarship to courtship, books to a beloved—sets the ethical groundwork for this love comedy.

Lucentio is observing the correlation between three concepts in these lines: philosophy, virtue, and happiness. Virtue and happiness are to be the subjects of his study. And—prior to Bianca's appearance, at least—he perceives that the *latter* (happiness) is only possible through the *former* (virtue). He also happens to believe that the particulars of these "virtuous deeds" lie between the pages of a book. *Study virtue, become virtuous, attain happiness* is Lucentio's initial plan. I suspect one of Shakespeare's jokes in *Taming* is that Lucentio will soon disguise himself as Bianca's tutor in order to woo her. And he'll never speak of virtue again. It's as though the play suggests there's no room for the education or the practice of virtue in relationship: by relinquishing scholarship for romantic love, Lucentio must *also* renounce his pursuit of virtue. He *will* attain happiness in love ("Happily I have arrived at the last / Unto the wished haven of my bliss"); but that happiness will be tinged with suffering. If you know the play's final scene, you know that Lucentio is humiliated in a bet when his assumptions about his new wife's obedience are proven wrong. ("The more fool you," Bianca will chastise him, "for laying [betting] on my duty.")

Buddhism might have suggested two things to Lucentio: don't quit studying entirely (though consider carefully your texts), and see that virtue is practiced *in relation*. "Virtuous" actions of body, speech, and mind are of utter importance in the Buddha's teachings, though Buddhism ultimately concerns itself with the development of a wisdom that transcends dualism ("rightness" versus "wrongness") and individualism (an "I" that develops personal virtues so as to treat "you" better). But while Buddhist ethics rest on an understanding beyond "me" and "you," this hardly means they're empty of relationship. Rather, when one sees the true nature of reality as Buddhism understands it, this radically changes our relationship to everything and everyone. Seeing the truth of nonself (*anatta*), for example, disassembles selfish motivations. Grasping the notion of rebirth (*punabbhava*, literally "becoming again") inspires us to regard each other as the grandparents, brothers, beloveds we've *been* to one another. Perceiving the nature of suffering (*dukkha*), we cease cleaving—as Lucentio has yet to learn—to our expectations about others. Virtue becomes so much more than Lucentio's accessory or adornment ("deck[ing] his fortune"). It's woven into the very fabric of our living because of what we understand of life. Rather than provide a formal set of moral rules, Buddhism invites us to ask ourselves in every next breath: Will *this* act of body, speech, or mind ultimately cause myself or others to suffer *more*, or to suffer *less*?

All of this is ultimately drawn from Buddhism's Eightfold Path (*ariya aṭṭhaṅgika magga*), more properly known as the

Eightfold Path to Happiness. It's encapsulated in the Fourth Noble Truth, and it covers the cessation of suffering. But while—like Lucentio—the Buddha called attention to the interdependence of happiness and virtue, he also taught that virtue is derived from *more than* Lucentio's scholarship ("philosophy"). This isn't to discount the meaningful role of study within the Buddhist tradition. But it *is* to say that our experiential knowledge of suffering—our being-in-relationship, whether with others or with ourselves—is just as critical to the practice and to the transmutation of that suffering into happiness. Lucentio's relationship with Bianca could indeed have been a fertile site for ending his own suffering.

Buddhism says that it's our present, moment-to-moment actions and intentions that determine our happiness: what we *do* rather than what's happened or been done to us. Mindfulness—the acute attention to one's experience in every next unfolding moment—is the foundation of the Eightfold Path. Engaged in the Path, the practitioner steadily inquires into the nature of mind and reality. He observes when he's sitting at the dinner table with friends, irritated and offended, having lost "a hundred crowns" because he expected his wife to be more dutiful than she is. (Bear with me; it's the play's strange example.) Perhaps he observes the patriarchal social conditioning behind his expectation. *Certainly* he asks: "*Who* is angry right now?" or "What is the suffering beneath my aversion (*dosa*)?" or "What if I sit with this displeasure until it—like all things—passes?"

Happiness is a state of mind, cultivated through discipline, that transcends the vicissitudes of our moment-to-moment emotional state. But we must track and inquire *into* those vicissitudes if we want to get beyond them. Happiness is more fundamental to Buddhism than many of us imagine, because we so often encounter the word *suffering* in its teachings. But it's what lies on the other side of philosophy—the love of wisdom, achieved through both the *scriptures* and *experience*, that produces a life of skillful action. Lucentio would call this virtue. Buddhism might simply call it understanding the nature of reality, and acting from that place.

THE NOBLE EIGHTFOLD PATH

"TO THINE OWN SELF BE TRUE": POLONIUS ON RIGHT VIEW

This above all—to thine own self be true,
And it must follow, as the night the day,
Thou canst not then be false to any man.

—*HAMLET*, ACT 1, SCENE 3

Polonius is perhaps the only character in *Hamlet* whose lines rival the prince's for recognition and admiration. His son Laertes is returning to school in France, and Polonius has just arrived to bid him farewell. Laertes has been exchanging parting words with his sister Ophelia; and when their father enters, the brother utters "a double blessing is a double grace": *what luck to have my father twice bless my departure.* It's a line typically spoken with a ring of sarcasm, and the best Ophelias look back at their brothers knowingly because they anticipate what's coming. After admonishing his son for his tardiness ("Yet here, Laertes? Aboard, aboard, for shame!"), Polonius goes on to delay him *further* with a series of precepts—injunctions to moral conduct—to carry with him back to France. The precepts concern integrity in thought, speech, action, and presentation; and they're recognizable to many of us by now ("Be thou familiar but by no means vulgar"; "Give every man thine ear but few thy voice"; "Neither a borrower nor a lender be"). But the three lines above contain Polonius's crowning advice. It's a call, "above all," to self-integrity.

Granted, this guidance on how to live expertly issues from a dubious character. Polonius is a busybody and a careful courtier who lives in a world of show; and these distillations of practical wisdom—sage as they are—are offered like a rehearsed string of clichés taken out of a schoolbook. I don't suspect Shakespeare intended to give Polonius much dignity or emotional depth in this paternal offering. Yet what his character lacks in substance his words atone for. *Be faithful to yourself, steadfast and unerring in who you know you are,* the precept urges. *Position your life so that it agrees with the standards you hold of yourself. And if you can do this, you will never be accused of insincerity or deceit.* On the surface it's a bit of a flowery tautology (saying the same thing twice): only be *true*, and you won't be *false*. Yet there's a meaningful causality here ("and it must follow, as the night the day") that posits the *self*—that is, our Buddha Nature, unclouded by defilements—as the origin and genesis of all-things-true.

One of Buddhism's principal teachings, and its Fourth Noble Truth, is the Eightfold Path: practical guidance on the cessation of suffering that extends back to the Buddha's first discourse. It's the antidote to the worldly knowledge we acquire—contained in the *First* Noble Truth—that suffering exists; and its elements are right view, right resolve, right speech, right action, right livelihood, right effort, right mindfulness, and right concentration. (By "right," think wise, skillful, or complete, rather than righteously "not wrong.") The eight precepts in Polonius's speech map rather magnificently onto the Eightfold Path, though that's an exercise for another time. *These* lines most closely echo "right understanding" or "right view" (*sammā diṭṭhi*): seeing things as they really are. "Right view is the forerunner of the entire path," Theravada Buddhist monk Bhikkhu Bodhi writes, echoing Polonius's "above all": "To attempt to engage in the practice without a foundation of right view is to risk getting lost in the futility of undirected movement . . . [like] wanting to drive someplace without consulting a road map or listening to the suggestions of an experienced driver."[47] *Without* right view, for example, one *cannot* produce right speech or right action. Polonius understood this in his "it must follow": the degree of our fidelity to the luminous self, the Buddha within, determines the flavor and tenor of the ways we are tender, or open, or wise, or kind to the world.

---

47 Bhikkhu Bodhi, *The Noble Eightfold Path: Way to the End of Suffering.* (Kandy: Buddhist Publication Society, 1998), 12.

The "understanding" of *sammā diṭṭhi* is best described as *inner* realization rather than the reception of wisdom from *outside* of us. The Buddha urged his followers to dispense with much of the external in their truth-seeking. He never intended for anyone to blindly adopt his teachings, but to take up the practice and judge for *themselves* whether or not they were true. In one story, the Buddha was passing through a village at a moment of tremendous cultural change and spiritual renaissance: many sages and ascetics were also passing through, preaching an array of philosophies and spiritual practices. The locals asked the Buddha how they could navigate the deluge of worldviews and opinions they were being inundated with. Which teachings were to be accepted and which rejected? "Don't go by reports, by legends, by traditions, by scripture, by logical conjecture, by inference, by analogies, by probability, or by the thought, 'This contemplative is our teacher,'" the Buddha replied. "When you know for yourselves that 'These qualities are unskillful; these qualities are blameworthy; these qualities . . . lead to harm and to suffering,' you should abandon them." Conversely, when they knew for *themselves* which qualities were skillful, blameless, and would lead to "welfare and to happiness," they should "enter and remain in them."[48]

It's just as precious advice for our twenty-first-century "social dilemma" of "choosing our own facts" amid a torrent of conflicting worldviews and opinions. In this sense, the "experienced driver" in Bhikkhu Bodhi's metaphor is *us, experienced.*

....
48 "Kalama Sutta: To the Kalamas," AN 3.65, Access to Insight, last modified November 30, 2013, http://www.accesstoinsight.org/tipitaka/an/an03/an03.065.than.html.

The road map is the internal compass we must be true to if we want to engage in the practice of life with direction. *Then* our knowledge is truly our own—and we are truly *ourselves*, in it.

So we might qualify Polonius's maxim: "to thine own *true* self be true." The practice asks us to continually discern between ego self (that loud, insistent voice conditioned by our *saṅkhāras*, our upbringings, our sociocultural influences, our social medias) and our Buddha Nature, our Luminous Mind, our wise and compassionate heart-self. The latter calls more powerfully and more articulately as we return, again and again, to listen and look within. *That* self is disclosed in the silence between incoming sound bites. And our faithful attention to what arises in those intervals allows us to cultivate relationships with *both* our selves: observing where they touch; where they disharmonize; how one, seen rightly, becomes an extended invitation to the other. And while it's unfinished work until we're fully awakened, we begin to distinguish between the cravings of the phenomenal self and our inherent and ever-present wisdom, the deep and abiding well within us.

Ultimately, this is a practice of exquisite and extraordinary trust: that the self we uncover through steady practice—the one *beneath* the posts and feeds and news clips and slogans and ego voices—is right and true. But when we find ourselves firm in that truth, we can be fearless in our faithfulness to it.

"THUS I LET YOU GO": MARK ANTONY ON RIGHT INTENTION

Look, here I have you; thus I let you go,
And give you to the gods.

—*Antony and Cleopatra*, ACT 3, SCENE 2

Mark Antony—one of three triumvirs who rule the Roman Empire—has been passing his time decadently in Egypt with its queen, Cleopatra, who's enchanted him away from his oligarchic duties. The disgrace and gossip Antony's "dotage" has occasioned have naturally given rise to tensions between the lover-general and Octavius Caesar, another triumvir, who's accused Antony of "giv[ing] a kingdom for a mirth." But when Pompey challenges the triumvirate's power, the men realize they can't defeat him without a stronger, more trusting alliance. Antony's sense of duty is awakened, and the suggestion is made that he marry Octavius's sister Octavia, "to make [them] brothers" and "hold [them] in perpetual amity."

And if a loveless marriage as a stratagem for resolving a handful of political rivalries sounds like a shortsighted idea to you, you know what's on the other side of this union.

Now, brother and sister are exchanging parting words. Octavius is not only grieved to see his sister go but also openly skeptical about the soundness of the bond he and Antony have forged. "You take from me a great part of myself," he tells Antony, referring to his sister. "Use me well in't." It's a remark that sits somewhere between caution and preemptive admonishment, and you might detect a shade of irritation animating Antony's response: "Make me not offended / In your distrust." Octavius turns to his sister to assure her he'll be thinking of her constantly. Eager, perhaps, to quit this atmosphere of suspicion—or impatient to return to his lover in Egypt—Antony interjects himself into the wake of Octavius's promise: "Come, sir, come, / I'll wrestle with you in my strength of love. / Look, here I have you; thus I let you go, / And give you to the gods."

It's a convivial-sounding challenge as to which of the two men loves Octavia more. But it recalls the underlying animosity between the triumvirs, and one can imagine a version of the scene in which Antony not-altogether-playfully pulls Octavius into a wrestling hold as he delivers these lines. But *however* tight you imagine Antony's grip on his fellow triumvir, you can imagine him embracing Octavius as he says "I have you" and extracting himself from the embrace as he says "thus I let you go."

I'm often struck by the word *thus* in this farewell hug. It's as though Antony is registering a natural and self-evident causality of having-then-releasing—or as though there was something fundamentally *un*natural about "having," or having for *long*. I have you, *therefore* I must let you go, the general seems to be saying—a remarkable thing to utter in a play about unhealthy attachment. I understand something of that "thus" in the second factor of Buddhism's Eightfold Path: *sammā saṅkappa*, right resolve or right intention. The Buddha described *sammā saṅkappa* as a threefold intention: the resolve to renunciation (which counters the intention of desire), the resolve to goodwill (which counters the intention of ill will), and the resolve to harmlessness (which counters the intention of harmfulness).

Repression was never a solution the Buddha offered. We don't resolve the "problems" of desire, ill will, or harmfulness through evasion or avoidance. Rather, the Buddha offered the tool of changed perspective, because we *are* what we *think*, and we *become* what we *intend*. "All experience is preceded by mind," *The Dhammapada* begins; it is "Led by mind" and "Made by mind."[49] One important practice for working with our thoughts is what we might call "thought substitution," applying an antidote. Contrary thoughts cannot coexist, so when one rouses thoughts and intentions of renunciation or nonattachment, they necessarily displace existing thoughts of greed. Likewise, thoughts and intentions of goodwill displace those of ill will; thoughts and intentions of harmlessness displace those of harmfulness. But *first*, one must observe the initial thought with compassion: "here I have you; thus I let you go." Bhikkhu

....
49 Gil Fronsdal, *The Dhammapada* (Boston: Shambhala, 2005), 1.

Bodhi uses a carpentry metaphor for the practice:

> The unwholesome thought is like a rotten peg lodged in the mind; the wholesome thought is like a new peg suitable to replace it. The actual contemplation functions as the hammer used to drive out the old peg with the new one. The work of driving in the new peg is practice . . . [for] whatever one reflects upon frequently becomes the inclination of the mind.[50]

In short, through a lifetime of patient practice, we gently push out intentions that lead to suffering with "right" ones.

Through the Four Noble Truths, and through sitting regularly with our own minds, we understand the nature of desire; we see how suffering arises from craving. When we understand *dukkha* as it pertains to our lives—that our fundamental wish is to be happy and free from suffering—it gives rise to that first intention: renunciation, nonattachment to the things of this world. When we apply that understanding to the lives of *others*—who share our plight of cyclic existence and who live with the same fundamental wish—it gives rise to the other two intentions: goodwill (the earnest and loving desire that they be peaceful, happy, and well) and harmlessness (the earnest and compassionate desire that they be free of suffering). This is how right view—which requires not only an honest exploration of our own internal landscape but also a capacity to enter into *others*' subjectivity and share their interiority— leads to right *resolve*. So we pick up the hammer and the pegs.

50 Bhikkhu Bodhi, *The Noble Eightfold Path: Way to the End of Suffering* (Kandy: Buddhist Publication Society, 1998), 38-39.

And our grip, *even* on our tools, is supple with compassion as we wield them to dislodge the thoughts that lead to suffering. As *The Dhammapada* says: when we resolve to change our *minds*, we change our *experience*.

Resolve is about more than deciding firmly upon a course of action, the fixing of a determination. It comes from the Latin *resolvere*: "to loosen, unyoke, undo, dispel, set free." By the late fourteenth century, the word had also taken on the sense of melting, dissolving, reducing to liquid. Each of these things has some relation to renunciation—Antony's "here I have you; thus I let you go"; the letting-be-water of all that's bound to trickle through our hands. Antony's can be a remarkably useful phrase when something is ending—whether a relationship or an experience that I'm not ready to part with, or a thought of ill will that I *am*. Granted, Antony and Octavius are hardly intimates in this play, so there's a lightness to Antony's words that I don't always have room for. But there's something about that second line—"[I] give you to the gods"—that helps us unclench our jaws and unfurrow our brows a little, as we loosen our embrace and open our hands.

UTTERING "SWEET BREATH": BOTTOM ON RIGHT SPEECH

. . . for we are to utter sweet breath . . .

—*A Midsummer Night's Dream*, ACT 4, SCENE 2

So says Nick Bottom—a weaver by trade and an aspiring-though-incompetent actor—to his amateur troupe of players (the "rude mechanicals") just before they perform for the Duke of Athens's wedding. In the hours leading up to these lines, the troupe had been distressed about their missing friend: "transported" by the fairies, Bottom had failed to return from the woods. They were *equally* concerned about their upcoming performance: Bottom plays the leading role, and because their friend has "the best wit of any handicraft-man in Athens," the show couldn't go on without him. Just as things begin to look worse for the mechanicals—Snug enters announcing that not only has the duke been married, but he's "coming from the temple" with "two or three lords and ladies more married," meaning the actors will disappoint *three* royal couples rather than *one* if they don't perform— Bottom returns.

Naturally, his friends are both overjoyed to see him and curious about where he's been. Bottom declares he has an incredible story to relate, though he equivocates about whether or not to tell it ("I am to discourse wonders; but ask me not what. For if I tell you, I am no true Athenian. I will tell you everything right as it fell out"). For *now*, there's certainly no time to narrate *anything*: the troupe must prepare to perform. "All that I will tell you," the reappeared weaver declares, "is that the duke hath dined": a signal that their performance is fast approaching. What follows is a speech that concerns material urgency: the players must "get [their] apparel together," string their false beards, ribbon up their shoes, and "meet presently at the palace." Bottom's final instruction to his "most dear actors" is to "eat no onions nor garlic" between now and the show. "For we are to utter sweet breath, and I do not doubt but to hear them say it is a sweet comedy." Beyond *that*, Bottom declares, "not a word of me."

There's much to unpack in this short scene about *whether* to speak, *what* to speak, and *in what time*. On the one hand, Bottom is constrained by present priorities, so he can't tell his story: the most meaningful speech he can offer is a catalogue of the mundane things the mechanicals must do to deliver a successful performance. On the other hand, one senses that Bottom declares "not a word" because what he's just experienced is incommunicable. His time in the bower with the queen of the fairies was an astonishing and ineffable dream. But of what *can* be said—indeed, what *must* be said, for the play must go on—"we are to utter sweet breath." Bottom is playing on a dual meaning of *sweet* here: pleasant to the *taste* and pleasant to the *ear*. It's part of his character's tendency toward synesthesia, sensory blending ("the ear of man hath not seen, man's hand is not able to taste . . . what my dream was," he's recently said). As though Bottom believes the gastronomical (*eat no onions*) could determine the linguistic and its reception (*so that your words please the newlyweds' ears, and tongues, and minds*).

Sammā vācā (right speech) is the third factor of Buddhism's Eightfold Path. It's also the first of the three factors on the "moral division" of that path (right speech, right action, and right livelihood) that cover ethical conduct and are the result of right view and right intention. The Buddha described *sammā vācā* as abstaining from four types of speech: (1) false speech (neither telling lies nor deceiving), (2) slanderous speech (not speaking in ways that create disunity, disharmony, or enmity), (3) harsh speech (not using impolite, abusive, or malicious language), and (4) idle chatter (not indulging in gossip or frivolous talk). We arrive at right speech through negation. What remains are words that are honest and sincere, that reconcile discord and soften what's hard, that nourish love, that are meaningful and benevolent, communicated at the right time and place, *on* virtue, *in* season. As the Buddha advised his followers: "When you get together, monks, only two things should be done. Either talk about the Dhamma [the Doctrine] or maintain a noble silence."[51]

....
51 N. H. Samtani, "An Abstraction of 'Silence of the Buddha: A Study into Philosophical and Sociological Aspects,'" *Buddha Dhyāna Dana Review* 7, no. 2 (1997): 70, http://www.bdcu.org.au/bddronline/bddr_1to10/BDDR07N2.pdf?x58958.

The beauty of *sammā vācā* is that it can be practiced every moment of every day—in the words we speak to ourselves, in the ones we extend to others, in the mindfulness with which we listen. We can set intentions at the beginning of each day to work on these four aspects of *sammā vācā*; we get instant feedback as our speech acts land on listening ears, and at the close of every day we can reflect on them. Were we truthful? Did we speak at the right time? Were we gentle or harsh, regardful or reckless? Were our words profitable? Did they sprout from the soil of *mettā* (loving-kindness), from a recognition of the Buddha Nature of every person we communicated with? Did they create or sustain harmony? Did we speak just to hear ourselves speak (or publicly post something just to see who would respond), so as not to get caught with ourselves in the silence? When we were silent were we *listening* or anticipating our next utterance? What did our silences express? If each of our "breaths" today was a seed (*bīja*), what will those seeds grow into?

Bottom is a fascinating case study in *sammā vācā*. He struggles initially to know *whether* he'll even speak, when it's time. But he recognizes that now isn't the time for past-tense narration: present-tense *living* must be tended to. He considers writing "a ballad of this dream," but even *that* will have its time and place: in the epilogue of a play, or at the fairy queen's death. Yet Bottom is as interested in the practice of silence as he is in timely speech. No matter how many times I come across this line, I'm always surprised by its final word. I expect to read "we are to utter sweet *words*" or "we are to utter sweet *sounds*." That *is*, after all, what an utterance is: an audible expression. Bottom's "utter sweet breath" is an invitation to notice the taste and tenor of silent respiration. (To "respire" is to return to life, which is what happens each time we recall the breath: its flavor becomes ever richer, more nectarous.) In the very presence of my mouth—even when it's not speaking a word—I'm "uttering." And there are ways of being *in* and *with* the breath that can make presence just a little sweeter.

"Do not speak unless you can improve upon the silence" is a phrase commonly attributed to the Buddha. *Sammā vācā* is a study in precisely this: letting the silence do its work and uncovering the most skillful ways to *add* to silence when speech becomes necessary. Conscious reflection on our speech clarifies the ways words become habits, makes us conscious of their consequences, and awakens us to the intricate and generous mystery of how words themselves can expand our hearts, can "sweeten" us.

"MY BODY SHALL MAKE GOOD": HENRY BOLINGBROKE ON RIGHT ACTION

. . . for what I speak
My body shall make good upon this earth . . .

—*RICHARD II*, ACT 1, SCENE 1

Richard II launches us right into an opening scene of ambiguity. Henry Bolingbroke, the king's cousin, is accusing Thomas Mowbray of treachery; King Richard is present for the allegation in order to arbitrate and dispense justice. One of Bolingbroke's accusations is that Mowbray was involved in the murder of Richard's uncle, Thomas of Woodstock. The irony here—the unspoken truth that everyone knows but no one dares to voice—is that Richard *himself* was a participant in his uncle's death. Bolingbroke knows that Richard ordered his uncle's murder; but having inherited convictions about the moral invincibility of the monarch, he can't accuse the king of such a deed. So he chooses the agent who did the king's dirty work as his target instead, putting both Mowbray and Richard in rather awkward positions: Mowbray can't blame the true offender because the culprit is the king, and Richard is now being asked to pass judgment on a crime that *he* engineered.

Mowbray denies each of Bolingbroke's accusations, and we never discover the extent of his guilt—though we *do* learn (and perhaps it earns him our sympathy) that Bolingbroke is beloved of nobility and commoners alike. And while both accuser and accused ultimately throw down their gages in this scene—a challenge to duel—they never physically fight. Richard exiles both men instead: this is *not*, after all, a quarrel the guilty judge wants to get caught up in. What we miss in this nonstarter of a duel, however, is how Shakespeare would've dealt with the assumption the language of this scene is soaked with: that the victor would be, *de facto*, the honest one. The very contest would prove—by virtue of who survived—which of the two men had spoken the truth. This is what Richard means when he says, at the close of the scene, "we shall see / Justice design the victor's chivalry." It's what Bolingbroke means when he claims that "What my tongue speaks my right-drawn sword may prove," and when he says to Mowbray—both incriminating him and threatening him to his face—"what I speak / My body shall make good upon this earth."

As a turn of phrase, "to make good" is to fulfill (as in a promise, an oath, an obligation, a threat), to carry something out successfully. It's a phrase Shakespeare used three times in this relatively short scene, beginning with Richard's initial question to Gaunt: Has he brought his son Bolingbroke to "make good" (publicly substantiate) the charges of treason he's made elsewhere against Mowbray? Bolingbroke's physical presence becomes a demonstration of his truth—indeed, a *precondition* for it. And for Bolingbroke, who's risking death to *prove* his truth, the body is an instrument that validates and substantiates the veracity and integrity of his words. Truth is verified in action. The word *good* conflates Bolingbroke's dexterity as a fighter (his ability to back up his words by force) with the moral integrity of his cause. And thus the phrase invites a secondary meaning: to "make good" is also to *produce* good, to be good's agent and originator. "Good" means an enormously broad range of things: favorable, desirable, beneficial, praiseworthy, virtuous, moral, righteous, complete. Bolingbroke's vow conveys that his body will create these things *in motion*.

Granted, Bolingbroke speaks these lines while "full of ire," and the debate never leaves the realm of words for that of action. But I love these lines because they marry *sammā vācā* (right speech) with the factor on the Eightfold Path that typically follows it: *sammā kammanta*, right action. Both are modes of being-with, of communing-with, of connecting; ideally they consistently communicate the Dhamma, the teachings. As with right speech, we arrive at right action through negation. The ethical precepts are perhaps the least equivocal aspect of Buddhist practice, and the tradition defines them with clarity: "abstaining from taking life, abstaining from taking what is not freely given, abstaining from sexual misconduct."[52] Buddhism maintains that these precepts are self-evidently good—though it certainly wouldn't say they're effortless or undemanding. Even so, they're the natural consequence of a person who understands the inexorable nature of cause and effect (*kamma*), non-self (*anatta*), and interdependent arising (*paṭiccasamuppāda*)—the idea that all phenomena are inextricably interconnected and arise in dependence of other phenomena. In other words, these ethical behaviors follow directly from right view (*sammā diṭṭhi*).

Rather than commandments or obligations to be fulfilled, the bodily precepts convey how a being should *naturally* move through the world and make action in it—compassionately, harmoniously, with love, and in reverence—when he realizes he's both owner and heir of his actions, inseparable from them, distinguished by them, made (and *made good*) by them. Buddhism suggests that practice *makes* integrity—"makes good," in Bolingbroke's terms. Right action is an organic consequence of mindfulness, reflection, and empirical understanding of the teachings. It's what, over time, our hearts will naturally prompt us to perform—sincerely, freely, as ourselves. So there's actually a great deal of freedom there, rather than restraint or prohibition. What happens when we marry these two meanings in Bolingbroke's oath, such that every action we resolve to fulfill or carry out will be a *good* one? Such that our bodies become instruments and architects of *goodness*?

....

52 John Haspel, "Magga-Vibhanga Sutta: Analysis of the Path," Becoming Buddha, accessed August 4, 2021, https://becoming-buddha.com/magga-vibhanga-sutta-analysis-of-the-path/.

"I HAVE IN THIS ROUGH WORK SHAPED OUT A MAN": RIGHT LIVELIHOOD IN *TIMON OF ATHENS*

I have in this rough work shaped out a man . . .

—*TIMON OF ATHENS*, ACT 1, SCENE 1

In the opening scene of *Timon of Athens*, an exchange between a Poet and a Painter takes place while both men—along with other merchants, artisans, and politicians—await the arrival of Lord Timon in a hall in his house. Timon is a wealthy philanthropist, patron of the arts, and exorbitant entertainer; and the artists have arrived in the hopes of selling the boundlessly generous nobleman their works. Timon's reckless liberality and his susceptibility to flattery will turn out to be his ruinous flaw: it won't be long before he's reduced to poverty through extravagance, at which point his fair-weather friends (the Poet and Painter included) will be exposed for the parasites they are.

In the meantime—and to pass the time until Timon's arrival—the men discuss the "gifts" they've brought their hoped-for patron, each commending the other on his art. At one point, the Painter observes of the Poet (who must be contemplating the lines he's written) that he's "rapt . . . in some work, some dedication / To the great lord." It's a remark that draws the Poet's attention away from his creation and back to the present moment. And it prompts him to describe his poem, at the center of which is a figure who resembles the very man—Timon—he's hoping to profit from by his verse. "I have in this rough work shaped out a man," the Poet begins: one whom Lady Fortune, enthroned on a hill, beckons to its peak "with her ivory hand" while all sorts of *other* men scramble up its sides to improve their fortunes. The tale-within-the-poem is a cautionary one about the fickleness of fortune: when the Timon figure "slip[s] down" the hill, not one of the "dependants, / Which laboured after him to the mountain's top" will support him. It turns out our Poet is a shrewd judge of human nature. And one wonders if he thought to represent *himself* among the hill-climbers in his own creation.

Right livelihood—*sammā ājīva*—is the fifth factor of the Eightfold Path, and the final factor (alongside right speech and right action) that concerns one's relationship with the external world. Specifically, *sammā ājīva* deals with "vocation" or "occupation" or "employment," though the definition of *livelihood*—the means of keeping oneself alive—extends far beyond our work lives. As with the other factors on the morality path, one can arrive at right livelihood through negation: abstaining from "business in weapons, business in human beings [slavery], business in meat, business in intoxicants, and business in poison."[53] Except as we practice it *today*, right livelihood isn't bound by this list. After all, the Buddha was addressing fifth-century Indian society in his teachings— herdsmen, farmers, traders. We have many more options, and much more to be mindful of, now.

The reason right livelihood is such a crucial arena for examining where our spiritual life meets our mundane life is that work takes up an enormous share of the latter. It's where we develop so many of our values and proficiencies and much of our intelligence. It's in large part where we self-actualize, what we set goals and aspirations around. Buddhism doesn't have anything negative to say about making money or about wealth, but it cautions against *earning* that wealth through harmful or dishonest means (see Timon's flatterers), against withholding its use for the well-being of others, against becoming attached or enslaved to it. Said in the *positive*, right livelihood is choosing to "make a living" (a phrase worth contemplating) in a way that's directly or indirectly beneficial to ourselves and to others, from a place of *ahiṃsā* (nonviolence), in an awareness that every sentient being is just like us in wishing to be happy and free from suffering. Or, as Thich Naht Hanh writes, "to practice right livelihood, you have to find a way to earn your living

....
53 "Right Livelihood: Samma Ajivo," Access to Insight, last modified November 30, 2013, http://www.accesstoinsight.org/ptf/dhamma/sacca/sacca4/samma-ajivo/index.html.

without transgressing your ideals of love and compassion. The way you support yourself can be an expression of your deepest self, or it can be a source of suffering for you and others."[54]

There are very few of us "householders" for whom the freedom exists to leave our jobs on philosophical grounds. (And even if we could, there's still a vast network of processes, activities, and human lives that sustains our existence. We can't circumvent those ties because they guarantee our *living*.) So many of our professions bear a burden of nagging doubt, even if only because withdrawing from the economic web they're woven into isn't possible. There are probably very few intrinsically pure vocations. Yet we crave careers that feel in integrity and alignment with our practice and our values, that nurture our own and others' well-being, that support our spiritual cultivation and our seeking. We want our mundane to meet the transcendent—because thinking of our worldly work and our Dhamma work separately reduces the latter to an extracurricular activity.

One approach is to view our work as more than a means of making a living. In Pāli, the word *sammā* means "rightly," but it also means "thoroughly." Because of the immensity of the systems that enfold our livelihoods—ones in which, unlike in the Buddha's day, a single activity impacts lives, lands, and ecosystems thousands of miles away—it's nearly impossible to adequately grasp the ripple effect of the work we do. But we *can* investigate the ripples closest to us and see if we can't get a

54 Thich Naht Hanh, *The Heart of the Buddha's Teaching: Transforming Suffering into Peace, Joy, and Liberation* (New York: Harmony Books, 2015), 113.

better view from there. We can keep our eyes, ears, and hearts open to the impact we're having on our employees, coworkers, clients, suppliers—all the way down the line—to understand not only the *consequences* of our work but also the activities and resources that *precede* it and make it possible. Does the sourcing of our materials show compassion for others and their communities? Does our offering lead our customers toward true happiness, or *away* from it? *Is* it an offering, in the most reverent sense of the word?

These kinds of questions form a mindfulness practice that shakes us out of autopilot. They prevent us from throwing ourselves unquestioningly into our work, but they also keep us from identifying with our roles too strongly. And as they widen both the lenses of our attentions and the horizons of our hearts, they wake us to the opportunities our jobs give us for kindness, service, and love. You may feel like there's nothing particularly spiritual or even meaningful about your job; yet *every* person, Buddhism teaches, is deeply interconnected. And the seeds (*bīja*) of action always bear fruit. Even the most mundane job becomes astonishing when we understand it as a series of opportunities to show others deep love and boundless compassion. And here is the "thoroughness" of *sammā* in *sammā ājīva*: one's livelihood examined as exhaustively as possible—*without* neglecting its tensions.

When the Painter observes that the Poet is "rapt" (enraptured, carried away) in the matter of his own livelihood, it recalls the Poet to the material moment, marrying the mundane with the transcendent. "I have in this rough work shaped out a man" is a rhetorical finger pointing to Timon. But the Poet has also shaped *himself* in the making of his "rough" (approximate, unfinished, imperfect) work. (Whether or not he's *honest* with himself in his poem is a thing we'll never know.) Our work *will be* imperfect, and it may only ever approximate the spiritual alignment we'd wish it to have. But if we can earn our daily bread while minimizing harm and maximizing regard, then we are indeed "shaping ourselves out" in "dedication"—not to an individual patron or boss but to all sentient beings we're in this interconnected web of keeping-alive with. When I make a question to myself of the Poet's line, it sounds something like this: What's the work I can do in *this* life, with *these* faculties, that will shape me most honestly into a figure of love?

"ALL LABOUR / MARS WHAT IT DOES": MARK ANTONY ON RIGHT EFFORT

Now all labour
Mars what it does; yea, very force entangles
Itself with strength.

—*Antony and Cleopatra*, ACT 4, SCENE 15

Mark Antony has been defeated by Octavius Caesar in battle: Cleopatra's ships "yielded to the foe," and Antony is initially furious at his lover's betrayal. The once-unconquerable general has become-stranger to himself in recent conflicts, and he's just described himself as a shape-shifting cloud to his attendant Eros: "That which is now a horse," "a bear or lion, / A towered citadel" in a moment becomes "indistinct, / As water is in water." It's an extraordinary image of essential formlessness, becoming-liquid, an arresting figure of water within water to express Antony's sense of lost identity. But just as we're reveling in the metaphor, Mardian enters with the news that Cleopatra has committed suicide. (Cleopatra hasn't, of course; but there's no reason for Antony to believe this is a strategy to turn his rage into grief.) The anguished lover instructs Eros to "pluck off" his armor, for he is "no more a soldier." That having been done, an armorless Antony soliloquizes how he will gather his remaining force for one crowning act. After all, now that Cleopatra is dead, "all labour / Mars what it does," and "very force entangles / Itself with strength."

The sentiment concerns the meaninglessness of existence without Cleopatra. But the language is so much more engaging than that. For one, Antony claims that all labor—all exertion, all endeavoring, all *doing*—obstructs ("mars") both the doing itself (the action) and what it does (the outcome). In other words, effort gets in effort's way. For another, "force" and "strength" are described as "entangled." Force and strength are synonymous—look up *force* in any dictionary and the first definition you'll likely see is "physical strength." The original sense of the root for *tangle* was "seaweed," which entangles something *other* than itself (think oars, fishes, or nets). Some editions of the play explain this line "as a powerful animal entangles itself in a net by the force of its exertion to escape."[55] But that isn't quite it. An animal and a net are two different things. But when "force entangles / *Itself* with strength" (emphasis mine) that's *self*-defeating action. Or, as Antony will

....
55 William Shakespeare, *The Tragedy of Anthony and Cleopatra*, ed. Michael Neill (Oxford: Oxford UP, 1994), 286.

shortly say—speaking as Cleopatra, whom he believes is now voiceless—"I am conqueror of myself."

Right effort—*sammā vāyāma*—is the sixth factor of the Eightfold Path. It belongs to the "concentration division" along with right mindfulness and right concentration. The Buddha taught that *sammā vāyāma* consists of Four Right Exertions: to prevent unwholesome qualities from arising, to extinguish unwholesome qualities that have arisen, to cultivate unarisen wholesome qualities, and to strengthen and perfect wholesome qualities that have arisen. The verbs (or their synonyms) are central to the point: *prevent*, *abandon*, *develop*, and *maintain*. *Sammā vāyāma* is active and rigorous; it demands our unfinished attention.

Buddhism offers a range of exercises for these endeavors. One can prevent unwholesome qualities by cultivating their antidotes, for example. Or one can arouse *wholesome* states through focus on the breath, which makes possible insight into the true nature of things by keeping one receptive to the present moment—stripped of commentary, interpretations, or projections. These unflinching investigations require our whole, effortful selves. But as contemporary Tibetan master Khenchen Thrangu Rinpoche notes, while the English *effort* carries connotations of drudgery, "in Tibetan the word for 'effort' has the notion of joy and enthusiasm."[56] Dhamma (the teachings) is for the diligent, not the lazy. Yet it's *joyful* effort

....
56 Khenchen Thrangu Rinpoche, "The Four Noble Truths and the Eightfold Path," Kagyu Samye Ling, accessed August 4, 2021, https://www.samyeling.org/buddhism-and-meditation/teaching-archive-2/kenchen-thrangu-rinpoche/the-four-noble-truths-and-the-eightfold-path/.

that allows us to engage in it—steadily, fixedly—for life. It's an effort that begets the energy for more efforting.

"Right Diligence is nourished by joy and interest," writes Thich Naht Hanh. "If your practice does not bring you joy, you are not practicing correctly."[57] The great Sri Lankan Buddhist monk and scholar Bhikkhu Pyadassi Mahathera writes of meditation (though it's applicable to all practices): "the technique is like that of . . . the sleeper—if you struggle with the thought of sleep . . . it will only be a mental torment to you. You must not make any effort to sleep. It must come naturally."[58] Contemporary British Australian Theravāda monk Ajahn Brahm distinguishes between "will power" and "wisdom power."[59] Will power fails to dispense with "me" and "mine," the desire for control and ownership; therefore it demands too much—and the *wrong*—effort. But "with wisdom power it's easy to practice right effort. . . . It's easy to abandon greed and anger, because [I simply see] they don't belong to me." And here's where right *effort* is only possible through right *view*: the understanding that nothing—not *even* the effort we put into the practice of right effort—belongs to us. As soon as we let go of "the controller," "the doer," "the one who is efforting," effort's been made "right." And the one who is appropriately efforting has the space to hear purely his *being*, because he's no longer attending to *doing*.

---

57 Thich Naht Hanh, *The Heart of the Buddha's Teaching: Transforming Suffering into Peace, Joy, and Liberation* (New York: Harmony Books, 2015), 100.
58 Bhikkhu Pyadassi Mahathera, "Buddhist Meditation," Buddha Sasana, accessed August 4, 2021, https://budsas.net/uni/u-thien-phatgiao/bud_med-1.htm.
59 Ajahn Brahmavamso, "Right Effort—Sammā Vāyāma," Dhamma Talks, accessed August 4, 2021, https://www.dhammatalks.net/Books7/Ajahn_Brahm_Right_Effort.pdf.

"Force entangles / Itself with strength" for as long as we keep trying to *do* the practice, since *doing* requires a subject—a self—which ultimately means more suffering. Instead, suggests Ajahn Brahm, "you just untangle and allow every thing to stop, to disappear."[60] I love Ajahn Brahm's verb here ("untangle"), because it's an undoing of Antony's *en*tanglement, a softening and surrendering and yielding that subtracts "us" from the equation so we can become water. Although Antony fears this dissolution of his identity, water is flexible, unresisting, accommodating. It does not strive; it does not overexert itself; it surrenders to natural forces rather than making-force. Yet over time it erodes even the hardest of materials. And in doing only what needs to be done and no more, it nourishes and benefits all things. When, through right effort, we become liquid like Antony's cloud, we do indeed become "as water is in water": indistinguishable from effort itself.

----

60 Brahmavamso, "Right Effort."

"I DO REMEMBER WELL WHERE I SHOULD BE": JULIET ON RIGHT MINDFULNESS

I do remember well where I should be,
And there I am.

—*ROMEO AND JULIET*, ACT 5, SCENE 3

Here's Juliet, on the verge of comprehending the tragedy she's in. She's just stirred from her "two-and-forty hours" sleep and is within her tomb, where Romeo and Friar Laurence were to meet her as she woke from a "borrowed likeness of . . . death." Of course, Romeo never received the letter from the friar—whose elaborate plan this was—explaining that his beloved is only in a deep slumber, not dead. And so—because he is a lover, and therefore fervid and impulsive—Romeo has already killed himself. Juliet is still coming to her senses and hasn't yet observed her lover's corpse, which is presumably close enough to be touching hers (after all, he died "with a kiss"). "O comfortable friar, where is my lord?" she asks of the Romeo whose body she fails to perceive. And then: "I do remember well where I should be, / And there I am."

The friar isn't exactly in a position to be "comfortable" (comforting) here. His strategy to unite the lovers has occasioned the deaths of two men—Romeo and Paris—and is soon to cause a third (you-know-whose). And in the context of the play, these lines are about resurrecting from an unconscious state—Juliet's had no pulse for two days—and the temporary disorientation of re-arrival into the world, the resuming of vital processes, of perception and participation after a profound absence. What I love about these lines is the causality they suggest: Juliet is present in memory and in mind *before* she is present in body ("I do remember . . . and [so] there I am"). Each of the three times she uses the first-person pronoun, the "I" feels more substantial, more awake, more present and sensitive to the world than the "I" that came before it.

Yet it's the word *should* that gives pause. For Juliet, rearriving to her body, "should" indicates correctness of location: she's been laid precisely where she needs to be laid for the plot to unfold as planned. Except it wasn't a *conscious* arrival: Juliet was out-of-body, literally asleep to her lover's "last embrace" and dying words. We could say that's the moral of presence in this tragic scene. And so to right mindfulness (*sammā sati*), the seventh factor on the Eightfold Path. The Buddha described *sammā sati* as cultivated through the Four Foundations of Mindfulness (*satipaṭṭhāna*): mindful contemplation of the body, feelings, states of mind, and phenomena. As with right effort, he offered a range of practices for these foundations. The *body* can be mindfully contemplated, for example, by making the breath an object of steady observation, grounding the practitioner in the present rather than roaming the labyrinthine past or future. It can be contemplated in its four basic postures—walking, standing, sitting, lying down—as well as in the transitions between them, which ultimately invites us to recognize the impersonal nature of our materiality. It can be contemplated as it performs *any* action: for example, Thich Naht Hanh's instruction to "wash the dishes to wash the dishes" rather than washing them "in order to have clean dishes."[61] It can be contemplated by mentally dissecting it into the four primary elements (earth, air, fire, water), recognizing they're the same elements that make up the external world and therefore ceasing to identify with it—since the body, like all else, is but a momentary configuration of changing material processes.

And so on with the other contemplations—of feelings, of states of mind, of phenomena. Is it a pleasant, painful, or neutral feeling that arises and now passes? Is it clinging, aversion or indifference that accompanies a given sensory perception? How does the water, the porcelain of the plate, feel on the skin of our hands as we're washing those dishes; and in what ways is it but earth and water meeting, for an exquisite flash, above that sink? What we discover, over time, through

....
61 Thich Naht Hanh, *The Miracle of Mindfulness: An Introduction to the Practice of Meditation*, trans. Mobi Ho (Boston: Beacon Press, 1976): 4.

mindful presence—"remembering well where we should be," then *being* there—is that mind and world are a stream of events that flicker into existence and are gone; we want to be wide awake to their fleeting loveliness. We get empirical insight into the nature of impermanence that dissolves greed, hatred, and delusion (*rāga*, *dosa*, and *moha*), because there's nothing of substance to respond to, to get involved in. And the more we observe, the less we relate to our thoughts and our feelings through habit. We can diffuse them rather than indulge them, since it turns out they're only discrete mental events with no permanent observer who's experiencing them.

Mindfulness is a noun, but it demands a great deal of verbing. Not *doing more*, but rather *un*doing our tendencies to project, associate, wish, judge, cling to whatever is happening. That's why mindfulness has a different tone and flavor than ordinary consciousness does. It invites us to suspend and surrender interpretations and judgments as they occur. It invites us to ask: "What is this thing *before* I name it, in the split second before it becomes the raw material for my mental commentary, my categories, for confirming my story?" The Buddha called this layering over of our own interpretations *papañca*—"embellishment" or "elaboration"—and it's worth noting the word *labor* in "elaboration": the excess work of not-letting-be. *Papañca* only ever lets us experience phenomena at a distance. Mindfulness, on the other hand, lets us access things *as they are*, in their immediacy and their miraculous wholeness. Fifth-century Indian Buddhist writer and philosopher Buddhaghosa describes it as "seeing the object face to face."[62] The contemporary Burmese meditation master Sayadaw U Pandita used the metaphor of "walking straight towards someone who is walking towards you."[63] This, truly, is the holy life—honoring every moment, and each of its parts, in its totality. Living deliberately and persistently in the abundant and generous present—each moment brand new, unconditioned by habit or reactivity.

If anything is to go well in *this* life plot, it'll be because we've been wholly attentive to its moment-by-moment unfolding. Because if we don't make conscious evaluations that lead us in skillful directions, we'll make *un*conscious ones, from "likenesses of death." And while the outcome may not look exactly like Juliet's, we might wake up one day and realize we've missed our window to alter the narrative or the touch of ardent love—the experience of which is only possible through our full-bodied, full-minded participation. So this is the mantra and the inexhaustible practice: to "remember well" to re-turn our minds to what's happening here and now, and invite our bodies to follow. The mind is powerful; our bodies won't require much urging. Even Juliet perceives this in the speed with which her presence follows recollection: "[Now] I do remember . . . And [now here] I am."

---

62 Quoted by Eric Harrison in *The Foundations of Mindfulness: How to Cultivate Attention, Good Judgment, and Tranquility* (New York: The Experiment, 2017): 152.
63 Quoted by Harrison, *The Foundations of Mindfulness.*

"CONTENT AND ANGER / IN ME HAVE BUT ONE FACE": ARCITE ON RIGHT CONCENTRATION

> *Content and anger*
> *In me have but one face.*

—*The Two Noble Kinsmen*, act 3, scene 1

The *Two Noble Kinsmen* is a play about two cousins— Arcite and Palamon—who are initially intimate and dear to each other but whose kinship is tested when both fall in love with the same woman (Emilia), abruptly making them rivals. The cousins have just encountered each other in the forest, where they've agreed that the only way to resolve their dispute is to fight for Emilia with swords—*Emilia's* desires, apparently, being irrelevant. But each has arrived to this confrontation from a different set of circumstances. Arcite has been serving the aristocratic Emilia in disguise and is living dignifiedly, in proximity to his beloved. Palamon, on the other hand, has just escaped from jail. Indeed, the latter is still in his shackles.

So for the first time in the play there's a marked difference in speech between the cousins, and the scene offers a contrast between the calm man and the passionate man that arises out of disparate conditions. As the cousin with the circumstantial upper hand, Arcite has the privilege of taking the high road in the conversation, maintaining a veneer of condescending honor and calling for chivalry in the face of Palamon's outraged suffering. The cousin in adversity finally tells Arcite to stop speaking so flatteringly ("be rough with me and pour / This oil out of your language"): *enough with the smooth words; meet me in my anger and in yours—because I know you're angry, too.* But Arcite won't use the rude language his cousin wants to hear. "Content and anger / In me have but one face," he replies. It's a comment on constancy: *I'm speaking to you in anger the way I'd speak to you in ease, with the very same expressions on my face and in my language.* The response is a continuation of Arcite's patronizing tone. (I don't suspect he'd claim "same-facedness" if *he* was the one in shackles.)

However you view Arcite in this scene, the single face that expresses sameness in both content and anger is a valuable practice. "Sameness" is the central feature of right concentration (*sammā samādhi*), the final factor on Buddhism's Eightfold Path. Though it's translated as "concentration," etymologically the Pāli word *samādhi* derives from roots meaning "to collect" or "to bring together." So we might define *sammā samādhi* as wholesome concentration—absorbed and singular focus on a salutary object—that unscatters the mind to unify it *on*, and ultimately *with*, its object. *Samādhi* collects our dispersed streams and tides of mental states into fixed and unbroken attention. What results in this attention is a tranquility sometimes called *upekkhā*, equanimity.

To emphasize, we're not talking just *any* kind of focused attention. As Bhikkhu Bodhi clarifies, neither "a gourmet sitting down to a meal, [n]or a soldier on the battlefield" is an example of *sammā samādhi*.[64] For one, the objects of concentration in these examples (dinner, the "enemy") are objects of craving (*rāga*) and aversion (*dosa*), respectively, meaning the concentration is not established in equanimity. What's more, the subject/object relation is central for both the gourmet and the soldier, but *sammā samādhi* is a state of awareness emphasizing neither subject nor object, because in the state of unified concentration, they become one. As Tibetan Buddhist meditation master Chögyam Trungpa writes, "Right absorption is being completely involved, thoroughly and fully, in a non-dualistic way. In sitting meditation the technique and you are one; in life situations the phenomenal world is also part of you."[65]

Which is why we must be very careful with what we choose as our objects of concentration. While single-pointed concentration on wholesome objects ultimately leads to unification and equanimity, the wrong objects become fetters.

....

64 Bhikkhu Bodhi, *The Noble Eightfold Path: Way to the End of Suffering.* (Kandy: Buddhist Publication Society, 1998), 86.

65 Chögyam Trungpa, *The Collected Works of Chögyam Trungpa*, vol. 3, ed. Carolyn Rose Gimian (Boston: Shambhala, 2003), 252.

Buddhaghosa listed forty proper objects of meditation (*kammatthāna*) in *The Path of Purification*. They include the four elements; death and decomposition of the body; and wholesome mental states such as liberality, peace, compassion, and equanimity itself.[66] Whichever of these objects the practitioner chooses, he focuses his mind on it and attempts to keep it there, steadily fixed and wide awake. If the mind strays, he gently-but-firmly brings it back, over and over again, as many times as is necessary.

The Buddha described *sammā samādhi* as occurring through four *jhānas*, levels or stages of meditation. They're exceedingly difficult to attain—certainly more so now, in our age of extreme distraction—but for meditators who reach the fourth *jhāna*, what remains is only that single-pointed attention within a field of neutral feeling, transcendent of worldly pleasure and pain. Consider an unflickering candle flame on a windless day or a pair of scales held, perfectly balanced, in a steady hand as appropriate metaphors for utter equanimity and unification. The meditator is unmoved, immovable, and undisturbable, experiencing without an "experiencer." The wave has remembered it's also the ocean and, in remembering, has dissolved back into it. What abides is an awareness that's beyond the dichotomy of observer/observed.

Of course, that doesn't mean the experience of equanimity is lost on those of us who never attain any of the *jhānas*. Cultivating equanimity through daily meditative practice

66 Bhadantācariya Buddhaghosa, *The Path of Purification (Visuddhimagga)*, trans. Bhikkhu Ñāṇamoli (Kandy: Buddhist Publication Society, 2011).

means the vicissitudes of life, over time, cease to unbalance our steadied scales so we can meet the world with greater degrees of sameness. And in the meantime, we can take up the practice of softening our faces—unclenching our jaws and unfurrowing our brows—when we come into contact with our "rivals." After all, if we soften our faces *first*, we might regard that which we're looking at with a little more softness. And somewhere in there we might realize that we're ultimately only looking back at *us*. What would it be like to go out with "one face" today—to maintain that singularity, that likeness of expression, no matter what we meet?

The Four Immeasurables

ARCITE'S PRISON COSMOS: EQUANIMITY IN *THE TWO NOBLE KINSMEN*

We are one another's wife, ever begetting
New births of love; we are father, friends, acquaintance;
We are in one another, families—
I am your heir, and you are mine . . .

—*THE TWO NOBLE KINSMEN*, ACT 2, SCENE 2

The story of the two cousins, Arcite and Palamon, continues—except we're now in the act *prior* to their heated forest encounter, where the two are imprisoned as war captives. This scene traces the arc of the kinsmen's dialogue from grief ("we are prisoners, / I fear, forever") to acceptance—and then pleasure—in their new circumstances. As the friends exhaust the catalogue of things they'll never experience as free men (to "feel our fiery horses / Like proud seas under us" or

"The sweet embraces of a loving wife / Loaden with kisses"), they begin to perceive something remarkable in the fact that "This is all our world. / We shall know nothing here but one another." Arcite proposes that the two will be as wives, fathers, friends, acquaintances, heirs to each other. Even as the cousins' world *materially* shrinks, it imaginatively swells with this abundant, omnirelational vision, emerging as a cosmos rather than a cell. Their prison becomes a "holy sanctuary": a site of the sacred realization that they're bound by a thousand ties.

Of course, we now know that the cousins will soon be estranged over a woman, and surely that's part of the irony of Arcite's declaration here. Scholars have struggled with the first line of that excerpt—"We are one another's wife"—which doesn't fit easily into the understanding of friendship in Shakespeare's time: the insinuation is too intimate even for an era that celebrated the deep and abiding affection that male friendship was founded on. But from a Buddhist perspective, this isn't an uncomfortable metaphor. In fact, meditating on the countless roles we've played across beginningless time allows practitioners to discover a state of equanimity (*upekkhā*) and affection in regards to *all* beings.

In the previous chapter we discussed equanimity as a state attainable through meditative concentration. It's also one of the Four Immeasurables (*appamaññā*) or *brahmavihārās*: sublime or divine abodes of Brahmā, a Vedic deity of the Buddha's time. You might think of them as godlike mindstates or virtues. They are equanimity, loving-kindness, compassion, and sympathetic joy. The Buddha's teachings on the *brahmavihārās* remind us that we are never *not* in relationship with one another. It might be easy enough to connect with these virtues on our meditation cushions, where there are fewer unsettling shocks and surprises to disturb us. But it's important that we bring these wholesome mental states into the world as well.

In seated meditation practice, *upekkhā* looks like inner equipoise as thoughts and emotions arise and fall away. We meet whatever arises in the mind on impartial footing; for the experiential wisdom of our practice—and of our lives—tells us they're but passing phenomena we just happened to get in the way of. In the context of our lives *off* the cushion, *upekkhā* is even-mindedness in the face of the Eight Worldly Conditions, life's vicissitudes: gain and loss, honor and dishonor, praise and blame, happiness and sorrow. It's the freedom to *not* ride the waves or the winds (pick your metaphor) of these changes but to be a rock unstirred by wind, as the Buddha poetizes it in *The Dhammapada*. And in the context of *relationship, upekkhā* meets all sentient beings impartially, irrespective of the present roles they play in our (present) lives. Equanimity is neither indifference nor apathy; it's the quieting of the mind that wants to categorize and identify with people as "friends," "lovers," "strangers," "family," "enemies." Ultimately, equanimity produces in us a warm benevolence toward *all* beings, because we feel as lovingly connected to them as to our family, our *saṅgha*, our circles, our intimates.

Upekkhā derives from a verb for "looking on" with a sense of dispassion. It deals in the wisdom and insight that comes with perspective, with seeing the bigger picture. As Thich Naht Hanh describes it, "You climb the mountain to be able to look over the whole situation, not bound by one side or the other."[67] Neither are we bound by *this* body, in *this* lifetime. The notion of rebirth—continuity across lifetimes—postulates that we haven't always been "us." We've been other people, other animals, other life forms, in other realms. Manifest in *these* bodies, we suspect that our relationships have some quality of fixedness. Those who are kind to us we call "friends," and we experience attachment and clinging with them. Those who are *un*kind to us we call "enemies," and we experience feelings of hostility toward them. Those who don't affect us either way we call "strangers," and we experience indifference or apathy with them. Wonder why you haven't been liberated? Buddhism asks. Climb that mountain; examine the situation thoroughly; check your relational categories. In fact we've been circling each other endlessly, and I've come close to you a hundred thousand times.

Recognizing—as Buddhism does and as Arcite suggests here—that we've played every imaginable role with each other levels the unevenness created in our minds by clinging and aversion (*rāga* and *dosa*). Of course, the relationships Arcite lists for his cousin here are all pleasing ones. But rebirth is generous in that it encompasses *all* forms of relation. That man beside you on the subway has been your beloved child. That person you refer to as your partner in this lifetime has

67 Thich Naht Hanh, *The Heart of the Buddha's Teaching: Transforming Suffering into Peace, Joy, and Liberation* (New York: Harmony Books, 2015), 174.

killed you in a previous one; those who mete out harm to you in *this* life have *saved* yours elsewhere. In his *Great Exposition of the Stages of the Path,* the fourteenth- to fifteenth-century Tibetan master Je Tsongkhapa quotes the *Sutra Requested by Excellent Woman Moon*: "I have killed you all in the past and you have hacked and cut me too. We have all been enemies and killed each other. [So] how can these thoughts of desire and attachment arise in you?"[68]

One meditation asks the practitioner to acknowledge that all sentient beings have been their mother. The story goes that the great sage Atisha, who helped bring Buddhism to Tibet, used to say "hello, mother" whenever he encountered another sentient being.[69] When we perceive that *all* beings have been selfless caregivers to us in the past, the impulse is to repay that kindness. We become deeply invested in their welfare. Meditating on others' "motherness" develops a recognition that everything that breathes, swims, runs, flies is an equally dear object of (our) affection. The difference between intimates, enemies, and those we overlook or see right past dissolves when we can see beyond the bounds of this lifetime. When "relationships" *plural* become a single *being-with*, across time, that affectionately binds us all.

From a Buddhist perspective—and in Arcite's words—we *have* known nothing here but one another. Whether or not

68 Quoted in Geshe Sonam Rinchen, trans. Ruth Sonam. "The Bodhisattva Vow," accessed August 4, 2021, https://www.shambhala.com/snowlion_articles/the-bodhisattva-vow/.

69 Thubten Chodron, "All Beings Have Been Our Mother," accessed August 4, 2021, https://thubtenchodron.org/2003/05/parents-importance/.

you believe in rebirth, in the beginninglessness of life, doesn't really matter. Buddhism says that the cashier at the grocery store has been your father, your cellmate, your mentor, your son. But even in *this* lifetime, he could easily become your brother-in-law or save your life. So whatever our beliefs, it's worth asking what we stand to gain by cultivating the recognition of others as our one-time mothers, most intimate friends, or brothers—even if it's only a metaphor for you, as it is for Arcite here. What changes when we take up Atisha's "hello, mother" or Arcite's "I am your heir, and you are mine" with every next encounter in this world?

LEONATO'S PROXIMATE HEART: LOVING-KINDNESS IN *MUCH ADO ABOUT NOTHING*

My heart is with your liking.

—*MUCH ADO ABOUT NOTHING*, ACT 5, SCENE 4

Leonato is the governor of Messina, and his house is the setting for most of Shakespeare's play. Both his daughter Hero and his niece Beatrice—a confirmed spinster who "cannot endure to hear tell of a husband"—live with him. When Leonato welcomes some friends home from war, among the party are two soldiers: Claudio, who is promptly smitten with Hero; and Benedick, who immediately resumes a longstanding "merry war" of insults with Beatrice. Indeed, the delight of *Much Ado* hinges on the comic banter and "skirmish[es] of wit" between these two self-professed enemies of love. But when Claudio and Hero are betrothed, the others decide upon a sport to pass the time before the wedding. They see that Beatrice and Benedick are made for each other and want them to stop bickering and bantering for long enough to fall in love. "If we can do this, Cupid is no longer an archer; his glory shall be ours," declares Don Pedro.

The game—which is successful from the first move—entails making both Beatrice and Benedick believe the other loves them, which naturally arouses in each a desire to *requite* that love. It's as though both characters need an invitation to contemplate being-loved by the other before they can acknowledge their own affection. That's not to say that either is willing to *concede* their newly kindled love: it's not until the lovers are caught writing secret love poems to each other ("A miracle! Here's our own hands against our hearts," Benedick exclaims) that they confess. When Benedick finally asks Leonato for permission to marry his niece, the governor responds with this most generous of yeses: "My heart is with your liking." *My soul, my will, my mind* ("heart" meant many things) *desires precisely what is pleasing to you.*

Mettā is the second of Buddhism's *brahmavihārās*. It's often translated as "loving-kindness": a warm, open-hearted goodwill toward all sentient beings, the wish that all of them everywhere have happiness and its causes. The emphasis, of course, is on the inclusive *all*; and it's worth distinguishing the "love" in "loving-kindness" from the way we tend to think of love. *Mettā* has no origins in affection or attachment. It's devoid of self-interest or the desire to possess—it recognizes, after all, that there is neither possessor nor possession. It has no conditions; it neither selects nor excludes. Instead it ripples out, washing over everything in its exuberant wake without expectation of anything in return.

Yet our intimate relationships are a starting place, because Buddhism says that the Four Immeasurables are qualities we *already* experience. Loving-kindness is not beyond us but *inherent* in us; we feel it for our children, our elders, our teachers. These are luminous glimpses into our ultimately limitless hearts, into the truth that love is potentially boundless. We can practice *mettā* exactly as we are; all we need is to desire for others what we desire for ourselves. *Mettā* practice progressively reveals to us that we can love with *wisdom* rather than with sentiment or attachment—without first evaluating whether someone is deserving, or useful, or pleasing to us. Wanting the person who cut us off in traffic this morning to be peaceful and fulfilled—to know love—is a viable and available wish. The same goes for our neighbor who cut down our favorite tree last week, the lover who was unfaithful, and the senator whose every legislative act we disagree with.

Buddhism honors the fact that we're each experiencing different forms of the same pain, and sorrow, and joy. One way of thinking about *mettā* is that it recognizes that all sentient beings can feel happiness and can suffer and that, given the choice, they'll choose the former. We know this best through our own lived experience, which is why *mettā* practice often begins with ourselves. In the Rājan Sutta (The King), the Buddha "exclaims":

> Searching all directions
> with your awareness,
> you find no one dearer
>   than yourself.
> In the same way, others
> are thickly dear to themselves.
> So you shouldn't hurt others
>   if you love yourself.[70]

The Rājan Sutta counsels us to extend the concern we already *have* for ourselves to others, because they, too, hold themselves dear. It resonates with the Christian injunction to "love your neighbor as you love yourself"—the implicit assumption being that we readily experience some form(s) of self-love. Of course, ultimately this isn't a chicken-or-egg argument (whom do I love *first*—others or myself?), because Buddhism tells you they're the same thing. One love is not a prerequisite for the other if you truly understand that you and your neighbor, "the other," are one. That's why I love Leonato's claim that "my heart *is with* your liking" (emphasis mine). It places two hearts beside each other—so close that they're nearly the same heart.

When one begins with oneself in loving-kindness practice, it's either to send loving-kindness *from* oneself *to* oneself or to imagine receiving it from another (a bit like the lovers in *Much Ado* are invited to contemplate being-loved by the other). You might think of these as self-addressed love poems: "May I be

70 "Rājan Sutta: The King," Ud 5.1, Access to Insight, last modified September 3, 2012, http://www.accesstoinsight.org/tipitaka/kn/ud/ud.5.01.than.html.

safe, may I be healthy, may I experience joy and ease"; "May I be free from inner and outer harm, light in body and spirit"; "May I move through this world contented, full, connected, and loved"; or whatever phrase speaks to your deepest desire in this life. We may initially feel self-judgment or self-hatred rising up against these self-blessings; but through practice, we drop *beneath* them to the place where we know tenderness for ourselves, where we care profoundly about our own well-being. Quoting the poet Galway Kinnell, Buddhist teacher Sharon Salzberg writes that "'to reteach a thing its loveliness' is the nature of metta."[71] While *loveliness* means beauty for us, in Shakespeare's day it meant "lovableness." To recall our lovableness is the greatest of rememberings, for we then have more available love for others—who *are* us.

Over time, we expand the circle—the field of the heart—sending *mettā* to someone it takes little effort to feel care and reverence for (elders, mentors, benefactors), then to those familiar and dear to us (family members, friends), then to neutral people (strangers), then to those for whom we feel resentment or hostile feelings, then to all sentient beings. We repeat the phrases we used on ourselves: "Just as I wish for myself, may you be filled with peace and happiness"; "May you move through this ever-changing world in health and joy, caring deeply for yourself as you go." In the moments we feel our hearts shut down—when we "meet" someone we can't yet include in the word *all*—we return to the previous recipient

....
71 Sharon Salzberg, *Lovingkindness: The Revolutionary Art of Happiness* (Boston: Shambhala, 1995), 22.

of our *mettā* and begin again there. Or we begin the phrase differently: "To the best of my ability, I wish for you . . ."

Mettā practice challenges us to be larger and more open than we thought possible. It's why the *brahmavihārās* are called "the divine abodes": extraordinary and expansive mind-states of the gods. To wish joy upon one who harms us—including the most hostile versions of *ourselves*—is among the most difficult of tasks. And while these wishes and blessings appear in practice to have a hierarchy ("me first"), my flourishing is yours; yours, mine. If I can touch the heart of every sentient being, I am touching—infinitely and unconditionally—my own trillion hearts. "My heart is with your liking" means I know that you, like me, will choose happiness over suffering—wholeness, love, and awe over grief and pain. Putting my heart beside, and in rhythm with, "your liking" is an act of seeing you in our semblance, an act of self-love in which "self" takes on its most expansive definition.

PROTEUS'S HOLY BEADSMAN: COMPASSION IN *THE TWO GENTLEMEN OF VERONA*

Wish me partaker in thy happiness
When thou dost meet good hap; and in thy danger—
If ever danger do environ thee—
Commend thy grievance to my holy prayers;
For I will be thy beadsman . . .

—*THE TWO GENTLEMEN OF VERONA*, ACT 1, SCENE 1

I n the opening scene of *Two Gentlemen*, Proteus bids farewell to his best friend Valentine. Valentine has resolved to go to Milan "to see the wonders of the world abroad," rather than "living dully sluggardized at home" as Proteus has determined to do. There's some good-natured chiding from one young gentleman to the other: unable to persuade his companion to join him, Valentine playfully suggests that Proteus runs the risk of "homely wit" (dullness) and "shapeless idleness" if he succumbs to the "chains" of affection he's bound by—a gentle mockery of lovesickness that can only occur between close friends. Indeed, Proteus remains in Verona because he's in love with a young woman named Julia, whom he hopes to woo while his friend ventures. Passion keeps Proteus home. And he isn't interested in defending himself against his friend's chiding. Rather, he asks Valentine to think of him, and with the above lines, commits to a kind of presence with his soon-to-be-absent friend.

The lines register the range of felt experiences we undergo in a life, from "good hap" to "grievance," exhilaration to anguish. Proteus's lines are a vow to be-with, despite not being physically present with his friend. To "partake" is to share in: *imagine me a participant in your joy when you're joying*, Proteus requests. *And when you're surrounded* ("environed") *by danger, commit your grief to the care of my prayers, for I will attend to the softening of your misfortune.* (A beadsman is one who prays for another.) *I want to be both "in attendance" (present) and "in attendance" (at your service) for every turn of the wheel of fortune that touches you.*

Granted, Proteus will go on to betray his friend: our youth has a lot to learn as the play unfolds. But what he promises in his "beadsman" remark—and what Valentine demonstrates when he forgives his treacherous friend—looks like *karunā*, the third of the Four Immeasurables. *Karunā* is typically translated as compassion, the wish that all sentient beings everywhere be free of pain and its causes—or in Proteus's words, the impulse to "partake" in their suffering. There are three ways in which *karunā* differs from ordinary compassion: (1) It experiences compassion neutrally, without *rāga* or *dosa*, like or dislike, for its object; (2) It feels compassion even for those who are happy, for it knows that the experience of suffering is rich enough to include the suffering within *pleasant* experiences (*viparināma dukkha*), occasioned by their impermanence; (3) It's active rather than passive. Genuine compassion, which recognizes that suffering permeates all existence, can feel uncomfortable. But that discomfort is potent and motivating; it leads to action.

To create the conditions for compassion, Shantideva writes, we must "strive . . . to meditate / Upon the sameness of [ourselves] and others."[72] For Buddhists, the practice of remembering that all beings have been our mother, brother, protector, lover through innumerable lifetimes is a helpful practice for *karunā*. Likewise, we've borne their *current* sufferings in bygone times; and if we can't learn compassion for them *here*, we'll be forced to learn it in some future rebirth. But even for non-Buddhists, it's a potent practice to remember that the goal of all sentient beings is our own. Even in the most trivial of daily activities, we're all trying to achieve freedom from discomfort and distress; we're seeking out peace and contentment. As Shantideva continued:

> And other beings' pain
> I do not feel, and yet,
> Because I take them for myself,

....
72 Shantideva, *The Way of the Bodhisattva* (Boston: Shambhala, 2007), 122.

> Their suffering is mine and therefore hard to bear.
> And therefore I'll dispel the pain of others,
> For it is simply pain, just like my own.

When we touch the wisdom that we're all one body, inter-dependent and connected to a whole, we cease to approach compassion unskillfully. We stop projecting our feelings onto those who are suffering, imagining how we'd feel if we were in their place. (There *is* no "our place" or "their place.") We stop confusing compassion with pity, which wants to remove suffering for selfish reasons (it doesn't want to look at it). And we stop talking about an "I" who feels compassion. There's neither a giver nor a receiver of compassion, nor is there a "gift" called compassion that passes between. There's only an unbinding-of-ourselves from ourselves that unblinds our eyes, undeafens our ears, and swells our narrow hearts as wide as the world.

One *karuṇā* meditation is called *tonglen*, a Tibetan term that means "sending and taking." As Pema Chödrön describes it, "tonglen reverses the usual logic of avoiding suffering."[73] Rather than acting on our knee-jerk reaction of turning and running from pain, we look at, connect with, and accept its presence. In this breath-based meditation, the focus is on whomever we've called up in our minds to extend compassion to. Inhaling, we breathe in the smoke and the pitch and the darkness of their suffering, visualizing them relieved of worry, or shame, or distress, or despair. Exhaling, we exude a

---

[73] Pema Chödrön, "Bad In, Good Out," Lion's Roar, October 2, 2017, https://www.lionsroar.com/tonglen-bad-in-good-out-september-2010/.

soft and quieting light, emanating like moonbeams—tender rays that touch the object of our meditation. Eventually, we expand the visualization to those experiencing similar griefs, then to all who are suffering—which is *every* being, which is (and includes) ourselves. The longer we practice *tonglen*, the less symbolic it feels. It's accompanied by the sense that we're literally transforming suffering into love.

One of my favorite ways to think about *karunā*—and *all* the Immeasurables, in fact—is that it's a practice of "making place" in my mind and heart for what's "else." This is different from trying to put myself *in* someone's place or *take* their place by suffering "for" them. It takes place out of the equation by clearing it. It recalls the fundamental emptiness we've arisen out of to become singular-but-interconnected beings, and that we'll return to to experience that sameness again. Proteus isn't claiming he'll *suffer with* in this promise to his friend. Rather, he'll make-place for Valentine's grievance in his own. He'll draw that grief up into his *own* prayer so his friend can release it a little, put it a little apart from himself. It's a dispersal of suffering into the whole so that no one has to carry it alone. Buddhism tells us that we're never carrying *anything* alone, anyhow. We just *think* we are—which, in and of itself, is a form of suffering worth having compassion for.

ROSALIND'S FORGOTTEN CONDITION: SYMPATHETIC JOY IN *AS YOU LIKE IT*

Well, I will forget the condition of my estate to rejoice in yours.

—*As You Like It*, ACT 1, SCENE 2

So says Rosalind to her cousin and inseparable companion, Celia. Celia's father has usurped his brother's dukedom, and Rosalind's father—the displaced and banished duke—now lives in exile in the forest. The usurping brother allowed Rosalind to remain at court, however, knowing that his daughter "would have followed her exile, or have died to stay behind her." Naturally, Rosalind is grieving her father's banishment; and as the scene opens, Celia—pleased that her best friend is still with her—attempts to cheer her ("sweet my coz, be merry"). Rosalind argues that she's *already* showing "more mirth than [she is] mistress of"; unless she can forget her father, she cannot "remember any extraordinary pleasure." So Celia turns the tables in a hypothetical scenario: if *she* were the one whose father had been banished by her uncle, she'd teach herself to take her uncle for her father (and thus, the logic extends, have nothing to grieve—for she would no longer be lacking a father). That's when Rosalind responds: "Well, I will forget the condition of my estate to rejoice in yours."

There are so many ways to interpret this line on the spectrum of sarcastic-to-sincere—though Celia *does* ultimately convince her cousin to "be merry." I love that Rosalind isn't professing to forget her "estate"—only its "condition"—as though she's willing to stand still ("to stand" is the root of *estate*) as external circumstances fluctuate, conditions come and go . . . which they *do*. And I appreciate the play on *estate*, which meant one's position in the social hierarchy but also one's situation generally. But what stops me every time is that word *rejoice*. While it means "full of joy," *rejoice* once meant "to own, to enjoy the possession of." In other words, Shakespeare is having Rosalind say: *I won't only joy in your joy as an outsider observing it; I will joy in* my *joy as well. Because your joy is mine as much as it is yours. It* becomes *mine by virtue of its very being,* regardless *of which one of us it touches first.*

This is *muditā* at its finest: sympathetic or vicarious joy, unclouded by self-interest, in another's well-being, happiness, achievements, or good fortune. *Muditā* is active joy in another's joy, delight in their pleasure *as if* it was one's own. Want a Christian equivalent? Look no further than the Apostle Paul's directive to "rejoice with those who rejoice" (Romans 12:15).

The boundlessness of *mudita* is that it doesn't care if we played a role in the other's happiness, and it joys with them *even as* we grieve our own tragedies and losses. Because it *joys*-with rather than *suffers*-with, *mudita* balances compassion (*karuna*), reminding the suffering heart that there's another side of the coin. It's worth noting that we have no one-word equivalent for *mudita* in English. We can only get there by pinning adjectives ("sympathetic," "vicarious") in front of the noun—as though *our* "joy" doesn't inherently extend to others. *Mudita* is traditionally understood as the most difficult of the sublime states to cultivate. Its hindrances—jealousy, envy, greed, judgment, cynicism, comparison—are many and powerful.

The reason it's so much easier for us to sympathize with others' misfortunes than it is to rejoice in their prosperity (just observe what gets covered in the daily news) is that genuine sympathetic joy demands a profound understanding of our interconnectedness. *Mudita* involves *upekkha* (equanimity) because it asks us to remember that we've been everything to one another and are boundless to each other. To rouse that sense of interdependence is to realize that there *is* no "diminishing supply" of happiness in this world, causing your bliss to impede mine. Nothing is taken from us when conditions give someone else pleasure, prosperity, or delight. When we remember that we're infinite, limitless as space—that, as in *As You Like It*, villainous uncles have been, and become, tender fathers—then the amount of happiness available to all beings also becomes infinite. Others' happiness *contributes* to ours rather than threatens it. And in lives principally characterized by suffering (as Buddhism understands them), we limit our opportunities to experience joy if we only delight in our own. When we delight in others' bliss as well, we exponentially multiply our occasions for joy.

The difficulty of *mudita* is why it's so important to deliberately cultivate the attitude, to create opportunities to experience it. We can develop *mudita* by pausing to appreciate the small joys of our own mundane yet astonishing lives—a practice that invites us to keep every sense open, tuning into joy as it arises. The flash of red on the bird outside your bedroom window, the way the coffee mug welcomes the flesh of your palm as though the ceramicist anticipated *your* particular hand, an important task accomplished, kind words from a colleague about the value of your work: each of these is an entryway to joy. (The poet Mark Nepo writes that "one key to knowing joy is being easily pleased.")[74] These focused attentions on wonder rewire our brains; and as we train the mind to give more weight to joy, we notice it arise more frequently in our lives.

In meditation, the method is similar to that of *metta*: "show up" first for your own joy, then for the joy of an intimate (can you joy in their joy unselfishly, without attachment?), then an indifferent person, then someone who frustrates or challenges you, then whole categories of beings—the happiness of new grandmothers, of lovers, of squirrels bounding between tree branches, of unleashed dogs encountering each other at

---

74 Mark Nepo, *The Book of Awakening: Inviting the Life You Want by Being Present to the Life You Have* (Newburyport, MA: Red Wheel, 2000), 23.

ocean shores. With the individuals you bring to mind, evoke their specific happiness or success as—like Rosalind—you make their "estate" your own. Visualize the facial expression, the gesture, that's their bliss. Your wish may be: "May your happiness not diminish" or "May your joy and good fortune continue forever" or "May you have even *more* joy—may you joy to overflowing."

To understand sympathetic joy as only relevant on the rare occasions when our loved ones experience windfalls is to fragment it and render it frivolous. Buddhism understands *muditā* as a quiet and ever-flowing inner spring of joy, not a tap we turn on periodically from which joy briefly gushes forth. Over time we'll observe that sending joy to others *doesn't* diminish our supply. That the more joy we share, the more joy fills us, self-replenishingly, until it boils up ebullient and flows out effortlessly. We "forget the condition of [our] estate" because we're drinking from the joy-spring that belongs to *all* of us, manifesting in one person's blessing before it vanishes and flashes up as joy in someone else—who is also us.

To forget our conditions we must set down "our" cravings, empty ourselves of self. Because it's the delusion of separateness—the misconception that *my* needs are in conflict with *yours*—that hinders joy. And when I can stop insisting I'm an individual, your joy is mine.

INTO THE
WORLD

"THE BEST CARDS FOR THE GAME": *KING JOHN*'S DAUPHIN OF FRANCE ON THE HANDS WE'RE DEALT

Have I not here the best cards for the game . . . ?

—*KING JOHN*, ACT 5, SCENE 2

Cardinal Pandolf has just arrived at the camp of Louis, Dauphin of France, who's at war with England, with a message from the pope: King John has submitted to the authority of the Catholic Church ("John hath reconciled / Himself to Rome"). This matters to the prince because his forces have been moving toward London with Pandolf's encouragement (you "thrust this enterprise into my heart," Louis will remind the cardinal). But this recent news is accompanied by an appeal that Louis withdraw his army and call off the expedition. It's a *volte-face* that hinges on his adversary's relationship with the pope: John now rules with the church's approval and under its protection. So Louis must "tame the savage spirit of wild war."

But Louis isn't having it. He won't be ordered about ("Am I Rome's slave?"); he reminds the cardinal that *he* was the war's first advocate ("Your breath first kindled the dead coal of wars"), and now it's got its own momentum ("'tis far too huge to be blown out / With that same weak wind which enkindled it"). What's more, he's heard the English shout "Vive le roi!"— "Long live the (French) king!"—as he's passed through their towns. "Have I not here the best cards for the game," he asks, reasoning aloud, "To win this easy match played for a crown? / And shall I now give o'er the yielded set?"

They're lines full of playing-card terminology: a "yielded set" was a game already won; a "crown" refers to the coin as a stake in a card game (as well as to King John's coronet, the symbol of sovereignty that Louis anticipates wearing); the phrase "Vive le roi!" was printed on sixteenth-century playing cards. In context, the dauphin is expressing an unwillingness to surrender what he believes is already *his*. But I love the card game as a metaphor for a life practice that dispenses with Louis's sentiments about wars and winning. Here we are, seated at the game table of life by virtue of having been born and, as Buddhism tells it, having already lived: dealt a certain hand (which we've dealt *ourselves* through prior existences), dealt new hands in each new breath while the cards we *just* held get dealt to others. This is what we have to play with. Nothing more. Or rather: nothing more than our world-making, game-making minds, which have us believe that there's only one table and that we're not *also* our opponents . . . and that the whole game—like England for Louis—isn't already *ours*.

For rather than imminent victory over an enemy (as it is for Louis), victory occurs for *us* the moment we look down at our hands—at those fragile but exquisite cards that make up our singular combination of conditions, traits, attributes, biologies, and genealogies *here and now*—and announce that we've been given the best possible cards to participate in, and play, this present life game with. We see all we've been handed—our joys and pains—as open doors to winning *everything*, which is everything we already have.

So how do we play our *current* cards such that we're decreasing the Three Unwholesome Roots (greed, hatred, delusion) and increasing the Four Immeasurables (equanimity, loving-kindness, compassion, and sympathetic joy)? Ultimately, we have a great deal of control over our present hands and how we play them. And this can profoundly reshape the subsequent hands we're dealt. Buddhism proposes a form of quite radical responsibility: we get the world we've created, and we *continue* to create it, now and into the future. Or to return us to the theater: we've been placed on a particular stage, with a rough outline of a script. Understanding that there are certain limitations and constraints, what role will we decide to play, while remembering that we're ultimately more-than-it?

Perhaps here, Shakespeare himself is our best guide. Within a small, rounded stage, well-worn stories, and theatrical conventions, he found enormous space: he found the Globe within himself. He tapped into an inner wisdom that still has us, four centuries later, searching and in awe of his language for what it can offer us about seeing *bigger*, and therefore living better. So we rise from our meditation cushions and head to the door to encounter the world in all its fullness, *as* itself. What shifts in us as we turn the handle and cross the threshold, perceiving the very bodies that step outside as the "best cards" with which to continue the inquiry?

BIBLIOGRAPHY

Acharya Shantideva. *A Guide to the Bodhisattva's Way of Life*. Translated by Stephen Batchelor. Dharamsala: Library of Tibetan Works and Archives, 1979. https://www.tibethouse.jp/about/buddhism/text/pdfs/Bodhisattvas_way_English.pdf.

"Adittapariyaya Sutta: The Fire Sermon." SN 35.28. Access to Insight. Last modified June 13, 2010. http://www.accesstoinsight.org/tipitaka/sn/sn35/sn35.028.nymo.html.

Ajahn Brahmavamso. "Right Effort—Sammā Vāyāma" Dhamma Talks. Accessed August 4, 2021. https://www.dhammatalks.net/Books7/Ajahn_Brahm_Right_Effort.pdf.

"Ananda Sutta: To Ananda." SN 44.10. Access to Insight. Last modified November 30, 2013. http://www.accesstoinsight.org/tipitaka/sn/sn44/sn44.010.than.html.

"Aññatitthiya Sutta." Buddhist Publication Society. Accessed August 4, 2021. http://www.buddha-vacana.org/sutta/anguttara/03/an03-069.html.

"Appamada Sutta: Heedfulness." AN 10.15. Access to Insight. Last modified November 30, 2013. http://www.accesstoinsight.org/tipitaka/an/an10/an10.015.than.html.

Bhadantācariya Buddhaghosa. *The Path of Purification (Visuddhimagga)*. Translated by Bhikkhu Ñāhamoli. Kandy: Buddhist Publication Society, 2011.

Bhikkhu Bodhi. *The Noble Eightfold Path: Way to the End of Suffering*. Kandy: Buddhist Publication Society, 1998.

Bhikkhu Pyadassi Mahathera. "Buddhist Meditation." Buddha Sasana. Accessed August 4, 2021. https://budsas.net/uni/u-thien-phatgiao/bud_med-1.htm.

Bloom, Harold. *Shakespeare: The Invention of the Human*. New York: Riverhead Books, 1998.

Bond, George D. "Theravada Buddhism's Meditations on Death and the Symbolism of Initiatory Death." *History of Religions* 19, no. 3 (February 1980).

Borges, Jorge Luis. "Everything and Nothing." Translated by J. E. Irby. Accessed August 11, 2021. http://www.friendsofcoleridge.com/ MembersOnly/Clayson_Ramsgate_files/borges.htm.

Buddhadasa Bhikkhu. "The Danger of I (Another Kind of Birth)." Dhamma Talks. Accessed August 4, 2021. https://www.dhammatalks.net/Books3/ Bhikkhu_Buddhadasa_The_Danger_of_I.htm.

Chödrön, Pema. "The Answer to Anger and Aggression is Patience." Lion's Roar. Accessed August 4, 2021. https://www.lionsroar.com/the-answer-to-anger-aggression-is-patience/.

Chödrön, Pema. "Bad In, Good Out." Lion's Roar. October 2, 2017. https:// www.lionsroar.com/tonglen-bad-in-good-out-september-2010/.

Chödrön, Pema. *No Time to Lose: A Timely Guide to the Way of the Bodhisattva*. Boston: Shambhala, 2005.

Chodron, Thubten. "All Beings Have Been Our Mother." Accessed August 4, 2021. https://thubtenchodron.org/2003/05/parents-importance/.

Chodron, Thubten. "The Three Forms of Generosity." Accessed August 14, 2021. https://thubtenchodron.org/1993/11/giving-material-aid-freedom-from-fear-dharma/.

Dass, Ram. *Paths to God: Living the Bhagavad Gita*. New York: Harmony Books, 2004.

Dass, Ram. *Polishing the Mirror: How to Live from Your Spiritual Heart*. Boulder: Sounds True, 2014.

"Dhammacakkappavattana Sutta: Setting the Wheel of Dhamma in Motion." SN 56.11. Access to Insight. Last modified November 30, 2013, http:// www.accesstoinsight.org/tipitaka/sn/sn56/sn56.011.than.html.

The Dhammapada. Translated by Gil Fronsdal. Boston: Shambhala, 2005.

Dogen. "Genjokoan." Translated by Reiho Masunaga. The Zen Site. Accessed August 4, 2021. http://www.thezensite.com/ZenTeachings/Dogen_ Teachings/GenjoKoan8.htm#clr0.

Epstein, Mark. *The Trauma of Everyday Life*. New York: Penguin Books, 2013.

Ford, John. *The Dramatic Works of John Ford*. Vol. 1. New York: J. and J. Harper, 1831.

Geshe Sonam Rinchen, trans. Ruth Sonam. "The Bodhisattva Vow," accessed August 4, 2021, https://www.shambhala.com/snowlion_articles/the-bodhisattva-vow/.

Goenka, S. N. "What Exactly Does 'Moha' Mean?" Vipassana Research Institute. Accessed August 4, 2021. https://www.vridhamma.org/node/2151.

Greene, Eric M. "The Dust Contemplation: A Study and Translation of a Newly Discovered Chinese Yogācāra Meditation Treatise from the Haneda Dunhuang Manuscripts of the Kyo-U Library." *Eastern Buddhist* 48, no. 2 (2017).

Hanh, Thich Nhat. "Dharma Talk: The Power of Visualization." Mindfullness Bell. Accessed August 1, 2021. https://www.mindfulnessbell.org/archive/tag/Eight+Levels+of+Consciousness.

Hanh, Thich Nhat. *The Heart of the Buddha's Teaching: Transforming Suffering into Peace, Joy, and Liberation. New York: Harmony Books, 2015.*

Hanh, Thich Nhat. *The Miracle of Mindfulness: An Introduction to the Practice of Meditation.* Translated by Mobi Ho. Boston: Beacon Press, 1976.

Harrison, Eric. *The Foundations of Mindfulness: How to Cultivate Attention, Good Judgment, and Tranquility.* New York: The Experiment, 2017.

Haspel, John. "Magga-Vibhanga Sutta: Analysis of the Path." Becoming Buddha. Accessed August 4, 2021. https://becoming-buddha.com/magga-vibhanga-sutta-analysis-of-the-path/.

"Hazlitt's Lectures on the English Poets." *Weekly Repertory, Or Literary Gazette* 3, no 2. Paris: Galignani's Library, 1818.

"Kalama Sutta: To the Kalamas." AN 3.65. Access to Insight. Last modified November 30, 2013. http://www.accesstoinsight.org/tipitaka/an/an03/an03.065.than.html.

Khenchen Thrangu Rinpoche. "The Four Noble Truths and the Eightfold Path." Kagyu Samye Ling. Accessed August 4, 2021. https://www.samyeling.org/buddhism-and-meditation/teaching-archive-2/kenchen-thrangu-rinpoche/the-four-noble-truths-and-the-eightfold-path/.

Khenchen Thrangu Rinpoche. *Instructions on Treatise entitled: 'A Teaching on the Essence of the Tathagatas (The Tathagatagarbha)' by the Third Gyalwa*

Karmapa, Rangjung Dorje, according to *An Illumination of the Thoughts of Rangjung Dorje: A Commentary to 'The Treatise that Teaches the Buddha Nature' by Jamgon Kongtrul Lodrö Thaye the Great.* Translated by Peter Roberts. Accessed August 13, 2021. http://www.dharmadownload.net/pages/english/Natsok/0010_Teaching_English/Teaching_English_0035.htm.

Kornfield, Jack. "The Beauty of Beginner's Mind." Accessed August 4, 2021. https://jackkornfield.com/beginners-mind/.

Lusthaus, Dan. "Vasubandhu." Accessed August 1, 2021. http://www.acmuller.net/yogacara/thinkers/vasubandhu.html.

Mark, Emily. "Wonhyo." *World History Encyclopedia.* Accessed August 11, 2021. https://www.worldhistory.org/Wonhyo/.

"Meditator's Toolbox: 21 Tips to Power Your Practice." Tricycle. Accessed August 4, 2021. https://tricycle.org/magazine/meditators-toolbox/.

Nepo, Mark. *The Book of Awakening: Inviting the Life You Want by Being Present to the Life You Have.* Newburyport, MA: Red Wheel, 2000.

"Pabhassara Sutta: Luminous." AN 1.49–52. Access to Insight. Last modified November 30, 2013. http://www.accesstoinsight.org/tipitaka/an/an01/an01.049.than.html.

"Phena Sutta: Foam." SN 22.95. Access to Insight. Last modified November 30, 2013. http://www.accesstoinsight.org/tipitaka/sn/sn22/sn22.095.than.html.

Rahula, Walpola Sri. "The First Sermon of the Buddha." Tricycle. Accessed August 4, 2021. https://tricycle.org/magazine/the-first-sermon-of-the-buddha/.

"Rājan Sutta: The King." Ud 5.1. Access to Insight. Last modified September 3, 2012. http://www.accesstoinsight.org/tipitaka/kn/ud/ud.5.01.than.html.

"Right Livelihood: Samma Ajivo." Access to Insight. November 30, 2013. http://www.accesstoinsight.org/ptf/dhamma/sacca/sacca4/samma-ajivo/index.html.

Salzberg, Sharon. *Lovingkindness: The Revolutionary Art of Happiness.* Boston: Shambhala, 1995.

"Sammaditthi Sutta: The Discourse on Right View." MN 9. Access to Insight. Last modified 30 November 2013. http://www.accesstoinsight.org/tipitaka/mn/mn.009.ntbb.html.

Samtani, N. H. "An Abstraction of 'Silence of the Buddha: A Study into Philosophical and Sociological Aspects,'" *Buddha Dhyāna Dana Review* 7, no. 2 (1997). http://www.bdcu.org.au/bddronline/bddr_1to10/BDDR07N2.pdf?x58958.

Shakespeare, William. *Antony and Cleopatra*. Edited by John Wilders. London: The Arden Shakespeare, 2006.

Shakespeare, William. *The Norton Shakespeare: Based on the Oxford Edition*. Edited by Stephen Greenblatt et al. New York: W.W. Norton, 1997.

Shakespeare, William. *The Tragedy of Anthony and Cleopatra*. Edited by Michael Neill. Oxford: Oxford UP, 1994.

Shantideva, *The Way of the Bodhisattva*. Boston: Shambhala, 2006.

Suzuki, Shunryu. *Zen Mind, Beginner's Mind*. ed. Trudy Dixon. New York: Weatherhill, 1995.

"The Three Basic Facts of Existence: I. Impermanence (Anicca)." Access to Insight. Last modified November 30, 2013. http://www.accesstoinsight.org/lib/authors/various/wheel186.html.

"The Three Basic Facts of Existence: III. Egolessness (Anatta)." Access to Insight. Last modified November 30, 2013, http://www.accesstoinsight.org/lib/authors/various/wheel202.html.

Trungpa, Chögyam. *The Collected Works of Chögyam Trungpa*. Vol. 3. Edited by Carolyn Rose Gimian. Boston: Shambhala, 2003.

"Vajracchedikā Prajñāpāramitā Sūtra," last modified October 30, 2020, https://en.wikisource.org/wiki/Vajracchedikā_Prajñāpāramitā_Sūtra.

INDEX

ACKNOWLEDGMENTS

Everyone who touches a life touches the work that emerges from that life; and there are countless encounters and embraces and laughs and loves between this book's lines. But gratitude especially to Patrick and to Sean, for your eyes and your wisdom and the tenderness with which you sat with this text in its forms. To Nicole, for confirming friendship across lifetimes by your very being. To Julieta, for your medicine and your heart. And to my Gassho companions, for the invitation and the ongoing encouragement to plumb depths I did not know were possible in this human form.

ABOUT THE AUTHOR

Lauren Shufran holds an MFA (Creative Writing: Poetry) from San Francisco State University and a PhD (Early Modern British Literature) from UC Santa Cruz. She taught a range of courses at UCSC—from *The English Sonnet Sequence* to *Biblical Poetics in Renaissance England*—but Shakespeare was the course she taught most often and most eagerly. She discovered yoga, meditation, and mindfulness practices while writing her dissertation.

Inter Arma (Fence Books), Lauren's first book of poetry, won the Motherwell Prize in 2013. Her poetry has appeared in Best *American Experimental Writing* (Wesleyan University Press), *Postmodern Culture*, *The Los Angeles Review of Books*, and elsewhere. She's also had scholarly essays published in *Renaissance and Reformation*, *Studies in Philology*, and elsewhere.

MANDALA

P.O. Box 3088
San Rafael, CA 94912
www.MandalaEarth.com

CEO Raoul Goff
VP Publisher Roger Shaw
VP of Creative Chrissy Kwasnik
VP Manufacturing Alix Nicholaeff
Editorial Director Katie Kilebrew
Associate Art Director Ashley Quackenbush
Sponsoring Editor Matt Wise
Project Editor Claire Yee
Editorial Assistant Sophia R Wright
Senior Production Manager Greg Steffen

Mandala Earth would also like to thank Ryan Pendell, Jessica Easto, Allie Kiekhofer, and Pilar Wyman.

Mandala Publishing, in association with Roots of Peace, will plant two trees for each tree used in the manufacturing of this book. Roots of Peace is an internationally renowned humanitarian organization dedicated to eradicating land mines worldwide and converting war-torn lands into productive farms and wildlife habitats. Roots of Peace will plant two million fruit and nut trees in Afghanistan and provide farmers there with the skills and support necessary for sustainable land use.

Manufactured in Malaysia

2025 2024 2023 2022 • 10 9 8 7 6 5 4 3 2 1